Dear Johnny

Johnny Carson's Most
Hilarious & Bizarre Fan Mail

Dear Johnny

Johnny Carson's Most Hilarious & Bizarre Fan Mail

Barbara Bowen and Mike Huber

Optima Books

Los Angeles San Francisco

Publisher: Optima Books
Editor: David Burke
Managing Editor: Robert Graul
Production: Optima PrePress
Overall Design: Richard Fire
Front Cover Illustration: Don Locke
Copy Editor: Janet Graul

Library of Congress Preassigned Catalog Card Number: 93-83817
ISBN 1-879440-15-6
Printed in the United States of America
93 10 9 8 7 6 5 4 3 2 1

This book is dedicated to…

Bubsy B. – Hang in there, kiddo! – Barbara Bowen

My mother and father for their constant love and support – Mike Huber

Foreword by Johnny Carson

During my nearly 30 years of hosting the "Tonight Show," I received literally thousands of marvelous letters, curios and elaborate gifts each week. Some of the most unforgettable have been included in this book.

"Dear Johnny" is dedicated to you, the viewers who took the time and the trouble to share their thoughts, their talents, and their fruitcakes!

Preface

It's difficult to even fathom how many pieces of mail Johnny Carson received in his nearly 30-year historic reign as host of the "Tonight Show." It's estimated nearly 20 million viewers tuned in every night to see Johnny, Ed, Doc and the band. When you think about it, no single television personality has had such a profound impact on our culture as Johnny Carson. The language of Johnny's "Tonight Show" has been integrated into the vernacular of us all. Watching the program was like being with an old friend; it was a comfort, something you could depend on. Many of the loyal viewers extended their "relationship" with Johnny by writing letters and cards, sharing their artwork, expressing themselves through poetry, or gifting him with anything and everything imaginable and indescribable. Along with the hundreds of letters and cards we opened on a daily basis, Johnny was sent enough clothing (and that included underwear... from both sexes... sometimes worn and dirty) to open an apparel store. We opened packages of food in every conceivable form ranging from snack items sent by reputable manufacturers to concoctions received from the home cook and baker in the hope that they could win over Johnny's heart with their culinary expertise. Some fans had no idea that their stewed tomatoes wouldn't travel well in plastic containers or that their homemade cookies or bread would resemble large clumps of dirt after the 2000-mile journey to Burbank. Every December, we were in receipt of nearly 60 fruitcakes. This, of course, in response to Johnny's on air chiding about those leaden holiday confections. Johnny was sent *objets d'art* by every level of artist (some couldn't wait for their canvasses to dry and mailed them in wet), and eccentric inventions and contraptions that would put Rube Goldberg to shame. Over the years, he was forwarded enough books to start a medium size library and literally hundreds of thousands of audio and video cassettes from "Tonight Show" hopefuls. Not a week went by without yielding golf and tennis equipment galore, new gadgets and toys, and literally everything from soup to nuts (we actually did receive hazelnuts resting in a small scale coffin, only to disappear one night, possibly eaten by the NBC night goblins).

Many will say it's a recent phenomenon, but there's always been a fascination with the world of the celebrity. It certainly has intensified in recent years due to the ever increasing number of media outlets, and the lust for celebrity scoops continues to grow. The voyeur in all of us is curious. Over the years many people have shown a fascination whenever we mentioned the amazing contents of Johnny Carson's fan mail. People generally want to know who would write to Johnny Carson? What do they say? What do they want? Why would someone send a cow dung clock to a talk show host? (Cow dung and other animal feces were popular items to send in.) Why do people take the time and the trouble to pour their hearts out and share things with Johnny that no psychotherapist will ever hear?

While "DEAR JOHNNY" is intended to be a lighthearted glimpse into the mail bag of the most famous television personality in the last three decades, it would be difficult to eliminate those letters written by people on the fringe of society. We do not mean to exploit these people, but to show an honest mix of the correspondence. Some letters are sincere in their praise or query, but many will confound or confuse, and some will even baffle the brightest among us. Hopefully, all the samples will entertain and give us some insight into the minds of the masses or at least those folks who watched the "Tonight Show" during Johnny Carson's astounding tenure.

Acknowledgements

- Our heartfelt thanks to David Burke for his vision, enthusiasm, expedience, and just about everything else.
- Our gratitude to Helen Sanders for her continual assistance and support.
- Gracias Sheila Wenz for the "bug in our ear."
- We're indebted to Kerry Lenhart for "that" phone call that eventually started the presses rolling.
- Merci Carol Katz for her friendship and constant reassurance.
- Much appreciation to Don Locke for his talent and patience.
- We want to thank anyone and everyone who helped to make "Dear Johnny" a reality.
- Lest we forget all those devotees, those wonderful eclectic fans who shared a part of themselves with Johnny over the years through the mail.
- And thank you, Johnny Carson, for your encouragement on this project, the wonderful foreword, and for nine years of steady employment in the most exciting environment anyone could imagine.

Note from the Authors

Photographs of the actual letters sent to Johnny Carson will be shown on the left-hand page with an easy-to-read *"translation"* on the right. As much as possible, we tried to reproduce the translations of the letters exactly as written, including misspelled words and incorrect use of punctuation. These errors will be indicated as follows:

[Mispeled] words will be shown like [thiis]

- Words surrounded by brackets indicate a spelling error made in the letter

Do you know Burt Reynolds[!]

- Punctuation marks surrounded by brackets indicate incorrect usage by the writer

My name is [ ] and I love your show

- To protect the identity of people mentioned in the letters, names and addresses in the translations have been replaced by empty brackets and blocked out in the actual letters.

Table of Contents

Table of Contents

Table of Contents

Dear Johnny

Johnny Carson's Most Hilarious & Bizarre Fan Mail

One of the *many* snapshots of outhouses sent to Johnny Carson bearing a *"Here's Johnny"* placard.

DEAR JOHNNY:

I am a very controversial figure. There seems to be a great deal of confusion as to whose birth certificate is mine and what kind of lifestyle I live. Perhaps you would like to invite me onto your program. I would be glad to try to answer whatever questions you care to throw at me.

Chapter One Make Me a Star

It's no surprise that the majority of people who wrote to the "Tonight Show" wanted to be *on* the "Tonight Show." You can't fault anyone for desiring their big break, their moment of glory, their brush with fame. Having talent was certainly no prerequisite for the hopefuls who sent in letters, audio and video cassettes, photographs, and books by the hundreds of thousands.

"I am a very controversial figure. There seems to be a great deal of confusion as to whose birth certificate is mine and what kind of lifestyle I live. Perhaps you would like to invite me onto your program. I would be glad to try to answer whatever questions you care to throw at me."

We were always on the lookout for interesting guests, people who did something highly unusual or who could be witty and entertaining to 10 million or more viewers. Although from time to time we would actually discover fascinating "civilians," most people just assumed that their 92-year-old grandpa would make a good guest simply because he made it to 92. Budding recording artists would send in homemade 45's, albums, or audio cassettes (probably recorded in their shower or basement) hoping to get national exposure and maybe even a record contract. We received a multitude of videos from all over the country featuring amateurs who sang, danced, did

4/22/91

Johnny Carson
Johnny Carson Show
No. Hollywood, Ca.

Is it possible I can come to your show? Theres is a man here that claims he has the answer to all the problems in the world. He has written to Pres. Bush, Jimmy Carter, Billy Graham & many others & no one answers his letters. So I'm writing to you so I can talk to you. I've watched you for 25 years so how do I get on your show. Maybe I'll have more luck with you. I have 125 patents & a job for every person in the United States. Please let me know when I can come and get on your show.

magic, told jokes, had their own local cable shows (even their own version of the "Tonight Show"), or had children or pets who performed. Some felt they would qualify as good guests because their friends thought they were entertaining and funny.

"Is it possible I can come to your show? There is a man here that claims he has the answers to all the problems in the world. He has written to Pres. Bush, Jimmy Carter, Billy Graham & many others & no one answers his letters. So I'm writing to you so I can talk to you. I've watched you for 25 years so how do I get on your show? Maybe I'll have more luck with you. I have 125 patents & a job for every person in the United States, Please let me know when I can come and get on your show."

One man wrote over 800 letters asking to realize his lifelong dream of taking Ed McMahon's place for one night just to announce, *"Here's Johnny!"* His persistence paid off when he was contacted by the "Tonight Show" producers who invited him to Hollywood to introduce Johnny the next week.

Those who were seeking their shot on the program spared no expense in decorating their envelopes and packages. We received elaborately ornamented parcels using every gimmick imaginable to attract our attention. Rarely would a day go by that a delivery of packages attached to enormous helium balloons wasn't sent to our office. Many fans sent their gifts and letters via certified or registered mail hoping we would open

DEAR MR CARSON AND MR MAH ON
POLL BETTS WOOD LIKE TO COME
TO THE SHOW AND SEE YOU?
WOOD YOU LET HAM BE ON YOU SHOW
HOPE TWO HEAR FROM YOU SOON

their letters immediately. We didn't. All mail was simply routed to the "in-box" and opened at random.

"Dear Mr Carson and Mr [Mahon] Pollbetts [wood] like to come to the show and see you? [Wood] you let [ham] be on [you] show hope [two] hear from you soon."

A Day in the Life of the Mail Room

The "Tonight Show" received a tremendous volume of mail each and every day. It was delivered at least three times a day and was stuffed into huge, unsightly cubby holes located in the lobby. On a typical morning, our talent coordinators would get a minimum of two newspapers including the Hollywood trade papers (the *Hollywood Reporter* and *Daily Variety*) and practically every magazine currently published; not to mention the plethora of submissions from agents, record and film companies (these usually included CD's, audio and video cassettes) along with press packages, news releases, books, and of course, letters.

The mail addressed to Johnny Carson was slotted in two places; one batch, which included his magazines, newspapers, inter-office mail from NBC, etc., went in one box, and the wide assortment of general fan letters addressed to the "Tonight Show," "Johnny Carson" or *Talent Coordinator Department* came directly to us. One of the most enjoyable and stimulating parts of the

Dear Sir,

I wrote to you last year about the fact I know 175 jokes, Well, I ~~know~~ now know over 200 jokes, If its ever possible to get on the show I would enjoy that, I raised 3 boys myself for over 7 yrs untill I re-married and never had the chance to be a comic, untill ~~b~~ now, but dont know where to start or have somebody to help me get started. But I know over 205 jokes and [illegible].

job was opening the tremendous number of submissions sent to the program by people from every walk of life, hoping for that big break. We were inundated by requests to be on the show ranging from the two-year-old tap dancing boy to the 107-year-old grandmother who wrestled alligators.

"I wrote to you last year about the fact I know 175 jokes, well, I now know over 200 jokes, if its ever possible to get on the show I would enjoy that, I raised 3 boys myself for over 7 years [untill] I re-married and never had the chance to be a comic, [untill] now, but don't know where to start or have somebody to help me get started. But I know over 215 jokes and building."

Working for the "Tonight Show" was a tremendous privilege. Not only was it the most renowned show in the history of television featuring an elite group of famous people, it was simply a wonderful and exciting way to spend a day. Our work hours were fabulous – 10:00 a.m. to 5:00 p.m. At 5:30 p.m. the show began taping, which we were always invited to watch. Who would want to miss it? We rarely taped on Mondays (3-day weekends!), except when we had a guest host (in which case we taped a full five days!) Music rehearsal began at 3:15 p.m. just about every day. It was the ultimate concert series – the perfect way to indulge yourself – not to mention getting up close to

My Dearest John,

I have really been waiting to hear from you, but I guess you are a little too busy to write me.

I really do care for you and since my love is so great, I shouldn't be suffering so much.

You see, I have this broken mandibul on the left side. I hope that I will have completely recovered by the first of January and, at which time I would like to appear on your show and sing like Sinead O'connor (Nothing compares). Please let me! I deserve a break and also, I have written two new songs I intend to record as soon as I am able. Please let me be on your show. I promise I will always respect you, your wife +

the biggest names in show business. It was hard not to get spoiled.

"My Dearest John,

I have really been waiting to hear from you, but I guess you are a little too busy to write me.

I really do care for you and since my love is so great, I shouldn't be suffering so much.

You see, I have this broken [mandibul] on the left side. I hope that I will have completely recovered by the first of January and, at which time I would like to appear on your show and sing like Sinead O'Connor (nothing compares). Please let me! I deserve a break and also, I have written two new songs I intend to record as soon as I am able. Please let me be on your show. I promise I will always repect you, your wife & children.

I hope you recall my letters, and I hope that we are really "close" to each other. I can dance a little, and I can really be a dramatic actress, or down right comic! Please give me a break. I am begging. I love you very much see [unnues] soon."

Though we were fortunate to have so many Mondays off, it meant the amount of mail that greeted us on Tuesdays was mind-boggling. On a normal day, the show would receive at least two gargantuan mail bags. Following the long weekends, the number would be five or more!

Each morning we picked up the mail in the correspondents' box and took it into our office to sort. Our first order of business was to scrutinize each letter

Mr. Johnny Carson
3000 West Alameda Ave.
Burbank, Ca. 91523

Dear Johnny:

This letter comes to you from a long-time admirer of your shows and the many talented people you have helped to get on in life. Ihave been told to try your show and see if I could get going to entertaining others. I'm not very much at doing things others have done but maybe you could toss a boquet on NBC and give the world some of whaT I have to offer. I shall list things that I can do. I knew nothing but Russian and Ukranian languages when I entered the first grade at [redacted] North Dakota. By the time I graduated from grade eight, I was hardly speaking anything but American English. Whan I was in my Freshman year there, I studied Latin and Caesar. Ultimately on getting my Senior diploma, I began to think of future things. I stayed out of school one year, taking Spanish by correspondence, following taking courses to become a teacher in science, among other studies.
I taught country school 5 years, spent summers in taking more education courses. I got my B.Science degree at [redacted] in 1964 at [redacted],including minors in Spanish, German, French, and more Russian. My grandfather came to America with the name [redacted] a name I found in a Russian Encyclopedia of a self-made field Marshall in the Cossack Army in Russia. I learned Norwegian from school bus drivers while at [redacted].So you can see I have had fun teaching and going to college for 35 years. I got my M,Music Ed. degree from [redacted] of Music,Chicago, had more ammunition for training high school bands, and choral groups in North Dakota, Michigan, Minnesota, Texas, Washington, Oregon, and California.

At the farm home near [redacted], we boys and my sister, gained experience at an early age in impersonating people. I can do Jimmy Stewart, very well,Buddy Hackett, Richard Nixon,John Wayne, Eva Gabor,Jimmy Carter,Ed McMahon,Matlock,Jonathan Winters, Henry Kissinger,Jimmy Stewart,Raymond Burr,Ed Sullivan,Yul Brynner,Elliot Ness.
I also do elephant call,why dogs growl. [I can do Amos,Andy,Kingfish and sing a bit of Negro spirituals like they would,but I would leave out what NAACP would not approve of]
I swim,dive,ski,like to fly. I've traveled to Europe,Much of U.S.A.,some of Canada.
I play piano,violin,clarinet,flute, and directed bands for 20 years. Could you arrange a small Ferris wheel to seat your band on to play Battle Hymn of the Republic, as the wheel turns, and include trumpet,trombone,tuba,and a sax player, with my directing this one number. Well, that is one idea I had my high school band do at a county fair in southern part of my state of North Dakota.

to determine whether or not it should go directly to Johnny's office. These included letters from other celebrities, entertainment industry-related companies, letters with impressive return addresses or those written on high grade paper with embossing, such as an invitation for a charity event; or maybe even a card from the White House.

Another multi-talented viewer seeking his fame and fortune. Sorry, we couldn't get the Ferris wheel through the stage door.

Determining what mail went where was just a sixth sense we developed. The mail had to be carefully screened each time we picked it up from our box. Letters or items going to Johnny's office had to be in his mailbox before 2:00 p.m., the time he usually arrived at the studio each day. There were certain things we knew he would want to see such as anything having to do with tennis, astronomy, and percussion. We went very few days without receiving something having to do with those interests. Because Johnny was so identified with his golf swing at the end of each monologue, viewers just assumed he was an avid golfer. We were sent a multitude of golf-related items when, in reality, tennis was his game.

After screening, came the seemingly insurmountable task of opening each and every piece of fan mail. It was actually impossible to open all the mail we received within just one day, so we were usually backlogged. As

Dear Tonight Show,

I have been writing you and sending you of my son [redacted] for about three months now. As you probably all ready know by now [redacted] is a magician and only I5 years old. He is called the court jester of magic because he combines comedy with his magic , you would have to see his show to appreachiate, his talnt,and that's why I have been sending you video's of his show but you just sent them back without watching them. He has literaly been told by every one who see's his show it was the best one they ever saw, and some them said "he's better then the one's we saw in Las Vages", and one time a man you was blind came up to him and said that's the best show I ever heard.

anyway, like I said I've been trying to get him on the show, I've even tried sending a certified letter to Johnny Carson himself but it was refused and sent back. Well this is going to be harder then I thought. So please could you send me information on how he could appear on the show , any thing would do just how to go about getting him on the show , if you could send me the names of the talent coordinators so could write to them .I know it is hard to beleive a mother but if you only could see his show ,he does a full hour production for his regular show but if he did appear on the show any time you give him will be just fine. He has appeard on the Disney channel but still one of his dreams is to be on the tonight show. well as I said any information you can send me on how to go about getting him on the show will be most helpful.

[redacted]

P.S. as [redacted] always says at the end of his show "if any of you want to see me on the tonight show all you have to do is ..... call them up and tell them about me.

we sat entombed behind walls of packages and envelopes, it was always amazing to us when fans called and asked if we had received their letter. We tried to explain that we received many thousands of pieces of correspondence each week, so it was virtually impossible to locate their single letter in the pile. Even then, some fans would insist that their letter should stand out since the envelope was pink (well, that at least narrowed it down to a mere *few* thousand). Fans always seemed astonished to learn their letter wasn't the only one received that week.

We always received letters from parents (and grand-parents) promoting their "gifted" children (and grandchildren) all hoping for them to have that big break by appearing on the "Tonight Show."

There were slots above our desks broken down by categories. As each letter was opened, we sorted it in the appropriate category to be answered at a later time. We tried to split the day by opening mail in the morning and answering it in the afternoon. The mail customarily tripled at Christmas and on Johnny's birthday when it seemed everyone in America sent a card. There was invariably an increase in the mail whenever there was a controversy which could be something whimsical discussed during the show, or a life-altering event that happened to Johnny. For instance, people wrote in for years in reference to the endless on-air argument Johnny and Ed had over the degree of intelligence of the pig versus the horse. It was

Johnny Carson Show   NBC Studios
3000 W. Alameda Ave.
Burbanks, Calif. #91523.

I would like to perform on the piano on the Johnny Carson Show. I would like to play a basa-nova, a jazz song, and a moody R & B. I studied piano at Zaph's Conservatory of Music, in Phila, from 1951 to 1955.
I would need a roun-trip ticket, by air, from Bangor, Maine.

Sincerely;

amazing how little gets past some people. A mis-pronounced word, a mis-stated fact, or a simple error in grammar was always enough to cause a sudden onslaught of letters and postcards.

No nonsense; to the point.

While there are so many experiences of our days in the correspondents' office to recount, nothing compares to the last month Johnny Carson hosted the "Tonight Show." It seemed like each day, there was an article, a magazine cover, or a story on the TV news about his pending retirement. There are few words to describe the stupendous outpouring of affection from Johnny's loyal fans. It was as if everyone on the planet was requesting a final autograph. People sent in their copies of "Life" and "TV Guide" magazines by the truck-load to be signed. The cards, letters, poems, gadgets, artwork and floral arrangements flooded our office to such a degree it was difficult to move around. The task seemed impossible; but we actually opened every piece of mail.

The Three Most Common Phrases Coming from Our Office

- "Why would anyone send this?"
- "We can't do this anymore."
- "EWWW! Get it away from me!"

Dear Johnnie:

Here are a few of the things I'd like to do on your show, with no one hosting.

1. Fitness song, especially the last verse in honor of our Flag.

2. A poem - Motor Complaints (in the voice of Jimmy Stewart)

3. A very short rendition of Adam and Eve in the Garden (in the voices of Eva Gabor, County Agent from Green Acres, Yul Brynner, and Richard Nixon)

4. Fast drawing of any person's profile in 12 seconds, with a Magic Marker

5. Bear in an apple, shown on photo

6. Born in the Navy, my own proof

7. Where God got the clay to make Adam

8. Why a dog growls

9. Conversation in Russian with you Понимаете ли вы?

10. Photo of our Turkey Quartet on the farm at Douglas, North Dakota

11. Photo of student-made toboggan or ski slide made of snow chunks on an area of a flat schoolground, at Calvin, North Dakota

Would you please take me on for at least the first five events?

The fitness song is about J. F. Kennedy; in verse 1, the Pacific Island boys rescuing him in the boat event, and the final verse with a new good meaning of what the colors of the United States Flag can inspire us as individuals to do.

Please write me or call me also as to the possibility of doing whatever possible on the Tonight Show. I sing bass in choirs.

Thanks a million for your doing.

Sincerely your friend,

The Most Mail Generated By a Single Event

We received the largest volume of mail after the tragic, premature death of Johnny's son, Rick. After this heart-rending event, letters poured in from parents who had also lost their children. Reading those tragic letters deeply touched our hearts and put life in its proper perspective.

When Did Mail Increase?

- Anytime Johnny was in the news or said something controversial on the show
- On his birthday
- During the holidays, especially if he mentioned fruitcake or discussed the pronunciation of "poinsettias" with Doc
- From the moment Johnny announced his plans to leave the show

Seems like just *too* much good entertainment.

The "Tonight Show" Switchboard

With nearly 20 million viewers each night, it's easy to imagine how many calls we would yield in a day. It's probably safe to say that second to the White House, the "Tonight Show" had one of the busiest switchboards in the United States (with some of the strangest incoming calls imaginable). The most common

Staff of Johnny Carson
3000 W. Almeda Ave.
Burbank, CA, 91523

Great Day;

Requesting personal review by Mr. Johnny Carson.

By the order of The Powers That Be... I have been instructed to apply for a band group guest performance on The Tonight Show.

Initial contact involved visionary communication link regarding such key words as " liquid string ". Do you give confirmation?

Requesting information regarding business procedure, involving legalities, ect.

questions were, of course, *"How can I get on the show?"* and *"Did you get my letter… I mailed it on Thursday."*

We certainly had our share of calls from guys in a bar making a bet with their buddies. They either wanted to brag that they just spoke to Johnny Carson's office or they had a $20 wager that 1962 was the year Johnny first hosted the "Tonight Show." People would call to complain about the previous night's monologue or to find out who was going to be on the show that night (or even six months down the road).

Many phoned in to request that Johnny interview particular celebrities (some of whom were dead!), or simply to give us jokes "for Johnny to use in his next monologue."

Aother request from someone, somewhere in our solar system.

It was not your typical switchboard. Each day at 2:00 p.m., a man would call and mumble about 15 words and then hang up. We had a woman who called every phone in the office and asked when her favorite dance team (Ron Eli and David Soul) would be booked on the show. We once received a call from a woman claiming to be Mrs. Carson (Johnny wasn't married at the time), and she wanted to know if Johnny and Ed were going out for drinks after the show. She needed to know what time to take the roast

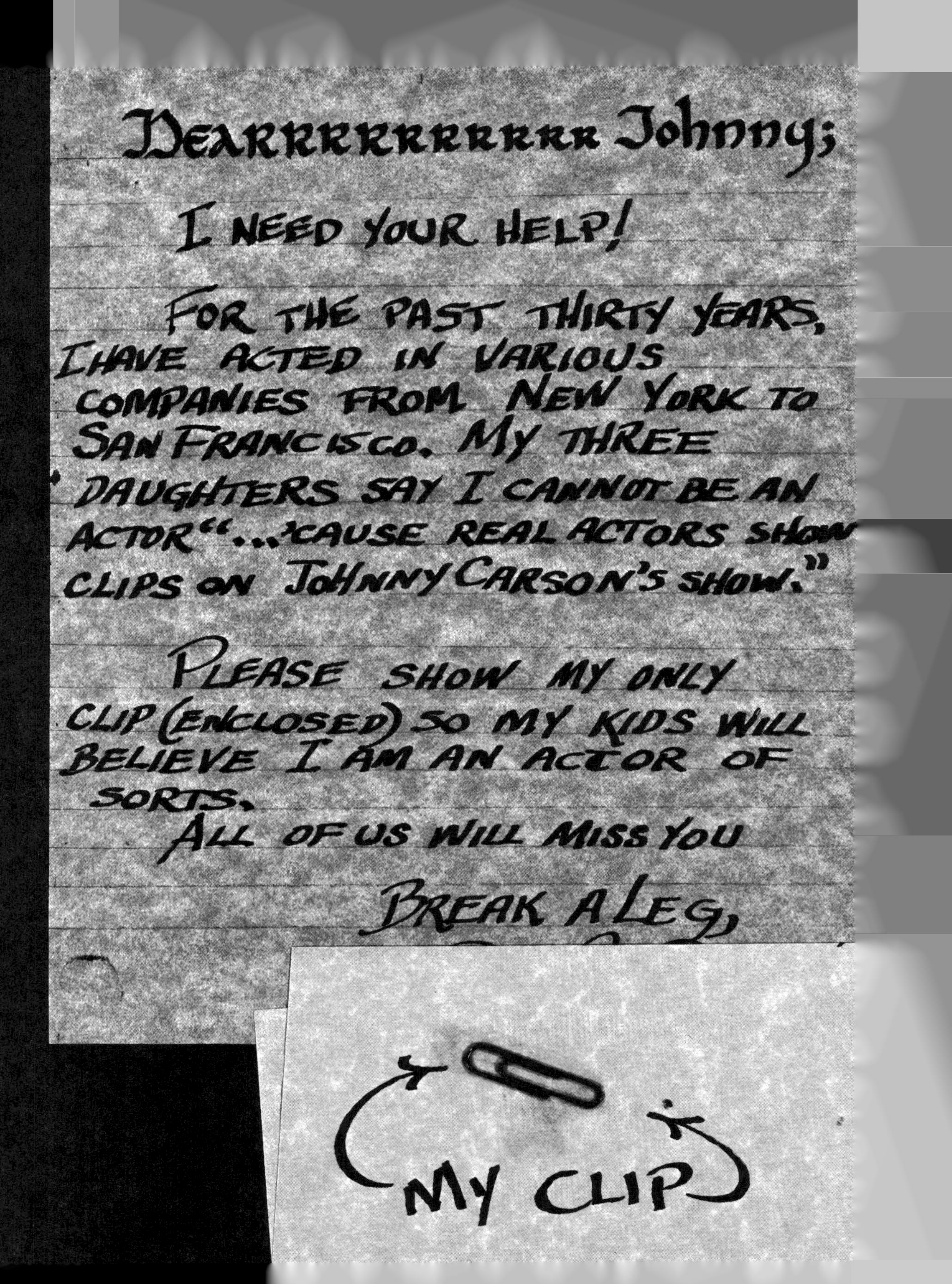

Dearrrrrrrrrrrr Johnny;

I NEED YOUR HELP!

FOR THE PAST THIRTY YEARS, I HAVE ACTED IN VARIOUS COMPANIES FROM NEW YORK TO SAN FRANCISCO. MY THREE "DAUGHTERS SAY I CANNOT BE AN ACTOR"..."CAUSE REAL ACTORS SHOW CLIPS ON JOHNNY CARSON'S SHOW."

PLEASE SHOW MY ONLY CLIP (ENCLOSED) SO MY KIDS WILL BELIEVE I AM AN ACTOR OF SORTS.

ALL OF US WILL MISS YOU

BREAK A LEG,

MY CLIP

out of the oven. She became very irate when we didn't put her through to Johnny.

From time to time, we got calls from those claiming to be God or Jesus. We always felt a little awkward asking them where they were staying so that Mr. Carson could get back to them. There were those rare calls when we thought some lunatic was pulling a prank, claiming to be the President of the United States, only to find that it really *was* the President (trying to reach our former head writer, who wrote material for George Bush). The largest number of calls was generated by the American Family Publisher's contest promoted by Ed McMahon. Some people actually flew all the way to Burbank because they really believed they had won.

Bah *dum* bum!

The day after we aired a segment during the holiday season showing new and unique products, countless calls poured in from viewers wanting to know how to purchase the items. People called about anything and everything that Johnny mentioned on the show. It was a very, very, very busy switchboard. Few employees, other than our regular receptionist, could handle the *"dreaded phones"* for more than an hour without losing their marbles.

Working with the Stars

Part of our job as a correspondent was to act as secretary to the guest host when Johnny was off. Prior to Jay Leno being named permanent guest host (after Joan Rivers left for the Fox Network), we worked for the following celebrity hosts:

- David Brenner
- Bill Cosby
- Billy Crystal
- Tony Danza
- John Denver
- Patrick Duffy
- Barbara Mandrell
- Garry Shandling
- David Steinberg
- Betty White

Jay Leno came in by himself, was pleasantly independent, and would balk at the idea of secretarial support.

Our Office

It was known as *"the fun place to be"* because it was like the yard sale of the absurd; the flea market of the bizarre. The bookshelves were perpetually filled with novelties, inventions, and boxes stuffed with books, audio and video cassettes. Our bulletin boards dripped with knickknacks and our desks were forever cluttered with coffee mugs and condoms. Portraits and pictures of Johnny lined all four walls of our office. There was a never-ending stream of staff parading through our office. It was the boredom breaker on those rare, dull afternoons when we didn't have a live show. Our fellow employees were constantly stunned at the diversity of decor; all thanks to the fans! About twice a year, the merchandise overpowered our work space and it seemed like the office kept on getting smaller and smaller. When we could no longer move around freely, we would call the hospital next door and donate the mountains of toys, T-shirts and trinkets… only to begin once again.

IT NEVER STOPPED!

Hi Johnny,

This is a very unusual letter but I just had to write.

On April 1 you ware a black tie with gold markings on it.

My husband [redacted] who recently had a bone marrow transplant, fell in love with your tie and said he would like one like it.

My reason for writing: Could you please let us know where I can buy this tie for [redacted] for Fathers Day? He has been in the hospital so much that I try to get him things that keep him happy.

We both love you
and will miss you
so much.

Chapter Two **Everyone Has A Request**

No appeal was too small, outrageous or unreasonable. The majority of those who wrote wanted SOMETHING. Many requested a signed photograph, tickets to see the show, the famous pencil with an eraser at each end, and especially, the coffee mug that sat on Johnny's desk bearing his picture. Interestingly enough, many viewers truly believed that Johnny could save their life, save the world, get rid of their warts or even loan them a necktie for a special event; not to mention redecorate their kitchen. "Send money, send clothing, send information, send us a part of you, Johnny Carson"... that was the universal summons.

"This is a very [unual] letter but I just had to write. On April 1 you wore a black tie with gold markings on it. My husband who recently had a bone marrow transplant, fell in love with your tie and said he would like one like it.

My reason for writing: Could you please let us know where I can buy this tie for Father's Day? He has been in the hospital so much that I try to get him things that keep him happy.

We both love you and will miss you so much."

Viewers constantly requested tapes of shows they had missed or which featured their favorite star. We had to explain that we didn't make tapes for sale to the public. Only guests that appeared on the show got a

Dear Daddy,

The real reason why I want to be on your show is I want to raise money. I'm a member of a club of ex-mental patients and we're trying to raise $50,000 for our new location for the kitchen alone. We're the Friendship Club in [redacted] [redacted]. Your consideration in this matter will be appreciated.

Sincerely,

[redacted]

copy and we kept a copy in our office for our records. This policy routinely met with great anger and disappointment.

"Dear Daddy,

The real reason why I want to be on your show is I want to raise money. I'm a member of a club of ex-mental patients and we're trying to raise $50,000 for our new location for the kitchen alone.

We're the Friendship Club in [ ]. Your consideration in this matter will be appreciated."

After A Long Day

Viewers continued to send us *letter-sized* stamped, self-addressed envelopes when requesting a signed 8x10 photo of Johnny. We were always tempted to take the photo and fold it to fit into the small envelope, but we never did.

Invitations

Fans of Johnny Carson routinely sent him invitations to their weddings, graduations, birthday parties, bar mitzvah's, picnics, family dinners, and backyard barbecues. He was in constant demand to speak at universities and to act as the Grand Marshall in a variety of parades. Invitations were sent from high school students requesting the honor of his presence at their June commencement as well as from the

Dear Mr. Johnny Carson and Mr. Ed McMahon,

I have some material that I think would make a movie equivalent to Gone With The Wind.

The listening devices have been on my mother and me since nineteen fifty six. Homes taken - Mail taken and mail boxes blown up. Cars torn up - Conversations gotten from car, home and telephone things stolen from residence.
Reproduced sounds caused my mother to have a heart attack. I was given treatment on false charges and something in my head burst and bled out through my left ear.
The people that are involved in doing all of that are police, family members, S.B.I. and F.C.C. - Also EX F.B.I. agent and Southern Bell Telephone Employees.

Right now it is in the hands of the F.B.I. Do either one of you know a super writer author or producer?

I have no money. Mother and I lost thousands of dollars - What you will do for me I will be eternally grateful.

President of the United States wanting him to attend a formal dinner. A "celebrity" is in constant demand.

"I have some material that I think would make a movie equivalent to Gone With The Wind.

The listening devices have been on my mother and me since nineteen fifty six. Homes taken – Mail taken, and mail boxes blown up. Cars torn up – Conversations gotten from Car, home, and telephone, things stolen from residence.

Reproduced sounds caused my mother to have a heart Attack. I was given treatment on false charges and something in my head burst and bled out through my left ear.

The people that are involved in doing all of that are police, family members, F.B.I. and F.C.C. Also Ex-F.B.I. Agent and Southern Bell Telephone Employees.

Right now it is in the hands of the F.B.I. Do either one of you know a super writer Author or producer?

I have no money. Mother and I lost thousands of dollars – What you will do for me I will be eternally grateful."

The Twelve Most Common Requests

1. To be on the show
2. Autographs (pictures, etc.)
3. Tickets to see the show
4. Personal items for celebrity auctions
5. The coffee mug on Johnny's desk or the pencil with double-ended eraser
6. Money
7. To participate in a business venture

Dear Johnny,

My husband & I got ourselves into a financial bind a couple years ago. Then my husband had to retire from the Air Force, where he was a Lt. Col. He couldn't find a job for several months, even though he's very intelligent, is very knowledgeable with computers, & has a Master's Degree in ~~Astronomical~~ Astronautical Engineering. He is now working for Met Life, but isn't making enough to pay our monthly bills. We're Christians, & we're asking God to help us out of this mess.

We read in TV Guide that you make $180,000 for each of your shows. We realized the salary from just one of your shows would get us totally out of debt, including our house. So how about letting us do one of your shows & getting your salary for it? Thank you.

8. Advice on life, love, and comedy careers
9. Did we mention money?
10. To wish a loved one "Happy Birthday" or "Happy Anniversary" on the air
11. To offer words of wisdom to institutions or organizations
12. Video cassettes of past shows

"My husband and I got ourselves into a financial bind a couple years ago. Then my husband had to retire from the Air Force, where he was a Lt. Col. He couldn't find a job for several months, even though he's very intelligent, is very knowledgeable with computers, & has a Master's Degree in Astronautical Engineering. He is now working for Met Life, but isn't making enough to pay our monthly bills. We're Christians, & we're asking God to help us out of this mess.

We read in TV Guide that you make $180,000 for each of your shows. We realized the salary from just one of your shows would get us totally out of debt, including our house. So how about letting us do one of your shows & getting your salary for it?

Thank you."

Celebrity Auctions

Every type of organization conceivable, from the "Save the Ferret Fund" to "The American Red Cross," wrote in requesting that Johnny send a personal item they could auction off to raise money for their cause. It was common to receive as many as sixty requests a day. Usually they were asking for a tie, a shoe, a hat, a cue card or the coffee mug that sat on Johnny's desk.

Burbank studios
attn: Johnny Carson
Burbank, California 91503

Dear Mr Carson:

I would like to make mottion Pictures. I lack a Personality so says the air Force although I take medication for this Problem. Please reply as soon as possible.

sincerely yours.

Sometimes the organization would request items to be autographed, such as a piece of fabric that would be sewn into a quilt. Since it wasn't practical to raid Johnny's closet, we opted to send a signed photograph instead.

"I would like to make motion pictures. I lack a personality so says the Air Force although I take medication for this problem. Please reply as soon as possible."

Send Money Right Away

We were both astonished at the number of people who wrote and freely asked for money. Many of these requests were certainly valid and understandable, but some of the time they were embarrassing. We had just opened a letter from a family needing money to help pay for the surgery of their sick child, followed immediately by a letter from a 23-year old man who wanted $23,000 for a brand new, red, Pontiac Trans Am!

One letter would break your heart and the next would try your patience. People wanted Johnny to pay their mortgage, their rent, their college tuition, their medical bills, and utility bills. It was even common to receive letters from fans soliciting money in order to buy a new seasonal wardrobe. Johnny Carson is a philanthropist, but it was impossible to fill the never-ending pleas for money.

Dear Mr. Carson,

I've been watching your program since the first night you were on and I'm sorry to see you leave. I'm not too well any more and T.V. means a lot to me. I'll miss you.

I feel like you've got more suits than you'll ever wear. I wear your size and if you ever get rid of some of them I'd sure like to have one. I'm seventy years old and never had an expensive suit like that.

Yours truly,

Protracted Appeals

- Jimmy Stewart once read a poem on the program about his dog named "Beau." This generated requests for copies of his poem for over *six* years.
- An inventor demonstrated his perpetual motion machine on the show. This single broadcast led to an almost daily 5-year onslaught of requests for his telephone number.

"I've been watching your program since the first night you were on and I'm sorry to see you leave. I'm not too well any more and T.V. means a lot to me. I'll miss you.

I feel like you've got more suits than you'll ever wear. I wear your size and if you ever get rid of some of them I'd sure like to have one. I'm seventy years old and never had an expensive suit like that."

Sharing

For some unknown reason, the public routinely sent Johnny:

- Their unpaid medical bills
- Copies of their prescriptions
- Their bank deposit slips

Dear Mr. Carson

While listening to your program on Jan [redacted] Tim Conway mentioned how to get rid of warts. I was just wondering if Tim Conway could tell me another way I might dispose of the wart as I live in Chicago and we haven't even seen the sun so far this month. If I have to wait until we get dew on the ground at 6 AM to rub my wart in, you'll be off the air and I'd be unable to contact you and let you know how things turn out, or how things drop off. Please let me know where I might write if either you or Tim Conway are interested.

Thank you

I wrote this [redacted] but didn't have your address until it showed up today in the TV Guide.

"While listening to your program on Jan [ ] Tim Conway mentioned how to get rid of warts. I was just wondering if Tim Conway could tell me another way I might dispose of the wart as I live in Chicago and we haven't even seen the sun so far this month. If I have to wait until we get dew on the ground at 6 a.m. to rub my wart in, you'll be off the air and I'd be unable to contact you and let you know how things turn out, or how things drop off. Please let me know where I might write if either you or Tim Conway are interested."

DEAR Johnny:

THE BROWN FELT HAT THAT WAS USED TO DRAW NAMES OF STUDIO AUDIENCE FOR GIVE-A-WAYS — IF NO ONE WANTS IT — I WOULD LOVE TO HAVE IT. GOING TO MISS YOU.

Century-old fruitcake remains in the family

TECUMSEH, Mich. (AP) — When Fridelia Ford died in 1879, she left behind an edible heirloom that has been kept in the family for more than a century.

The family treasure is her last fruitcake, made in November 1878 in her Berkey, Ohio, farmhouse.

"The tradition was that they baked the cake on Thanksgiving, let it age for one year, and then cut into it the next Thanksgiving," explained Morgan Ford, her great-grandson.

When Fridelia died the next spring, the Ford family preserved her memory by keeping the rum-flavored fruitcake. Morgan Ford has been its custodian since 1952.

"I keep it in the dining room, kind of up high where the grandkids can't get to it," he said.

Twenty years ago, Uncle Amos Ford nibbled on the family treasure — with permission, of course.

"We like to say that he lived for two years more, so it couldn't have been too bad," Ford said.

Ford took over guardian duties after his father died. He said he intends to pass it on to his own son, James.

The fruitcake sometimes accompanies Ford to family reunions, where the youngsters have the chance to get acquainted with family legend. But no one in the Ford family is making future heirlooms.

"We buy 'em. We don't make them," Ford said.

Pigs Have Warm Smiles

CHAMPAIGN (AP) — Stanley Curtis' pigs may not understand the energy crisis, but they are doing their part to conserve fuel.

They flip a switch in their pens to turn on the heat only when they are uncomfortable. And, evidently, they will turn off the heat when they are warm enough.

If preliminary results are verified, it could mean farmers will spend less to heat hog houses, and pigs will be happier and more productive.

Curtis, an animal science professor at the University of Illinois, has been experimenting with the pigs and the heat in their pens for four years.

"We became interested when the energy crisis began," Curtis said. "We thought that we might be keeping the hog house warmer than the pigs wanted."

Young hogs cannot tolerate low temperatures, and farmers in cold climates must add heat to hog houses in the winter months.

The pigs in the experiment quickly learned that a switch in their pen turned on heat lamps.

"They operated the switch more often — twice as often — in the daytime than at night," said Curtis. "They were wanting a warmer environment in the middle of the day than in the middle of the night."

That could save a farmer money on his fuel bills.

"The brown felt hat that was used to draw names of studio audience for give-a-ways – if no one wants it – I would love to have it. Going to miss you."

JOHNNY,

I WAS WONDERING WHAT YOU LOOK LIKE WITHOUT YOUR SPORTSCOAT.

GOOD LUCK,

"I was wondering what you look like without your sports coat. Good luck."

Johnny Carson

NBC_ TV

3000 Walameda Blvd .

Burbank , CA 9152 3

Dear Johnny :

I would like all the free info you have . Thanks .

Respectfully ,

Perhaps they should purchase an encyclopedia or a good dictionary.

N.B.C. TELEVISION
BURBANK, CA.
JOHNNY CARSON SHOW

DEAR JOHNNY,

I AM WRITING TO ASK YOU A FAVOR. I REALIZE YOU ARE GOING TO RETIRE VERY SOON (MUCH TO OUR DISMAY). BEFORE YOU GO I WANT TO ASK YOU WHAT YOU INTEND TO DO WITH THE COAT AND HAT YOU WORE WHEN YOU WERE IN THE SKIT ABOUT THE DUMB FARMER. I HAVE A FRIEND WHO WANTS A C.C. FILSON JACKET SO BAD AND IT IS RED WITH THE BLACK LINES JUST LIKE THE ONE YOU WORE. IS THERE A POSSIBILITY I COULD BUY THAT ONE FROM YOU AND GIVE IT TO MY FRIEND THE CONSERVATION OFFICER IN OUR COUNTY???? I KNOW HE WOULD APPRECIATE IT VERY MUCH AND I COULD TELL HIM IT WAS GOOD ENOUGH FOR JOHNNY CARSON SO IT'S GOOD ENOUGH FOR HIM.

THANK YOU VERY MUCH. ANXIOUSLY AWAITING A REPLY

Appeals like this were commonplace. Once a woman wanted a dress a female guest wore on the show so that she could wear it to her daughter's wedding. Folks wanted to raid Johnny's closet as well as those of his guests.

Dear Mr. Carson

I tape your show every night and watch it at breakfast in the morning. I'm a domestic goddess so I have nothing better to do than write letters to people I don't even know.

I'm writing to ask you to give Carl Reiner a polygraph test. About three appearances ago he asked you for a souvenirr. The first thing he grabbed for was your cigarett box but you talked him into taking a pencil instead.

The next week you went on vacation and when you came back the cigarett box was gone. Your prop man took the blame but I think Carl paid him off.

The next time Carl was a guest on your show he brought souvenirs and memorabilia of famous deceased actors so I think he really does collect things of famous people and I can't see you retire without reopening the case of the missing cigarett box and give Carl Reiner a polygraph test.

Sincerely

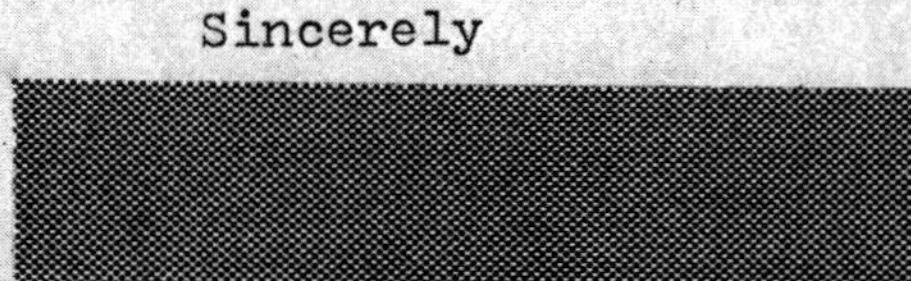

We tried not to submit our guests to polygraph testing.

Dear Mr Carson:

I know you're going to be retiring soon but I was wondering if you could do something before you leave your show. Sort of a public service message. This has sort of bothered me for years. The queen of England. She waves wrong. Am I the only one who noticed? Even as a child she sort of holds her arm out and twirls her wrist like a helicopter propellor. It's not right. She may not know shes doing it wrong. Someone may have showed her this way as a joke and no one ever had the nerve to correct her. She seems a nice lady. She deserves to be told she waving wrong. If she drove by a group of school kids doing this they wouldn't know what she was doing. Maybe while she's brushing her teeth or rolling her socks into little balls for the next day she'll catch you're message out of the corner of her eye. Who's it gonna hurt. The worlds got enough problems without the queen waving like Trixie from the Honeymooners.

Sincerly

Chapter Three **People With Opinions**

Those with strong convictions often chose Johnny as the target of their "venting." By writing, they could cleanse their emotional palate. No subject was too trivial or remote. Angry viewers got a chance to air their beef while more mild-mannered people, simply made wardrobe suggestions. One thing is for certain, people are passionate.

"I know you're going to be retiring soon but I was wondering if you could do something before you leave your show. Sort of a public service message. This has sort of bothered me for years. The queen of England. She waves wrong. Am I the only one who noticed? Even as a child she sort of holds her arm out and twirls her wrist like a helicopter propellor. It's not right. She may not know she's doing it wrong. Someone may have showed her this way as a joke and no one ever had the nerve to correct her. She seems a nice lady. She deserves to be told [she] waving wrong. If she drove by a group of school kids doing this they wouldn't know what she was doing. Maybe while she's brushing her teeth or rolling her socks into little balls for the next day she'll catch you're message out of the corner of her eye. Who's it gonna hurt. The worlds got enough problems without the queen waving like Trixie from the Honeymooners."

We think the Royal family has enough problems right now. Let's not burden them any further.

True Confessions

Who needs a shrink when you can just write to a celebrity and share your deepest thoughts and feelings? We read letters about personal loss, financial struggles, loneliness, despair, and unrequited love. We received

Dear Johnny Carson:

I'm an 81 year old seamstress. I thought I'd write with a suggestion on how to improve on your clothing appearance. I can't watch all your shows as at my age I have to retire early most of the time. I watched your

This is what I saw, you wore a gray suit top and sandy colored trousers. Your suit top and many of them as I have seen have split sides to accomodate your hands going into your pockets. The thing which irks me is when your hands are in your pockets, the white lining weaves about like a diaper and distracts me. I think your top suits coats should be lined to coordinate with the color of the top suit, meaning if the suit is gray the lining should also be gray perhaps a lighter or darker gray I'm not sure, let your tailor decide. It could be a pretty lining with gray stripes or whatever.

Ages ago there was a style where mean had a pleat in the back of a BLACK top coat and it was white. My husband had such a top coat & I hated it. Every time he made a move the white lining would show. What I did I sewed 2 pieces of black cloth at the triangles & it solved the problem. Perhaps your tailor could do the same to some of your remaining top suits so as not to show off the white color like a diaper.

patches over white.

open vent in back center

patches to cover white

Sincerely,

an abundance of multi-page letters that just tracked the day via a stream of consciousness as if Johnny were their diary or journal. These letters contained some of the most personal information imaginable which we were always stunned to see being divulged to a stranger.

"I'm an 81 year old seamstress. I thought I'd write with a suggestion on how to improve on your clothing appearance. I can't watch all your shows as at my age I have to retire early most of the time. I watched you [ ].

This is what I saw, you wore a gray suit top and sandy colored trousers. Your suit top and many of them as I have seen have split sides to accomodate your hands going into your pockets. The thing which irks me is when your hands are in your pockets, the white lining weaves about like a diaper and distracts me. I think your top suit coats should be lined to coordinate with the color of the top suit, meaning if the suit is gray the lining should also be gray perhaps a lighter or darker gray I'm not sure, let your tailor decide. It could be a pretty lining with gray stripes or whatever.

Ages ago there was a style where men had a pleat in the back of a black top coat and it was white. My husband had such a top coat & I hated it. Every time he made a move the white lining would show. What I did I sewed 2 pieces of black cloth as the triangles & it solved the problem, Perhaps your tailor could do the same to some of your remaining top suits so as not to show off the white color like a diaper."

Believe It or Not...

People actually counted:

- How many times Johnny touched his tie during the monologue
- How many times he licked his fingers to turn pages (we received lots of rubber finger protectors)

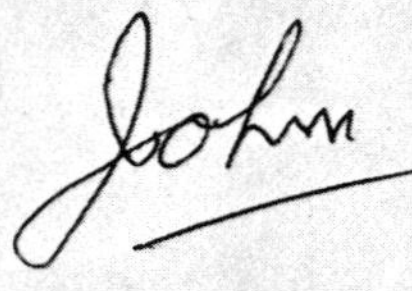

I WISH YOU WOULD GIVE THAT SIDE KICK OF YOURS A FEW EXTRA BUCKS. IT SEEMS TO ME HE NEEDS IT.

EVERY TIME I TURN ON THE TV OR RADIO HE TRYING TO SELL SOMETHING. FIRST HE WAS SELLING MAGAZINE SUBSCRIPTIONS & GIVING AWAY $10 MILLION DOLLARS. NOW HE IS SELLING LIFE INSURANCE. FIRST THING YOU KNOW HE WILL BE SELLING "CONDROMS" IT A BIG THING HERE IN NY

TAKE CARE OF HIM SO HE CAN SPEND HIS LATE YEARS RELAXED WITH A FEW DRINKS INSTEAD OF RUNNING FROM ONE STUDIO TO ANOTHER MAKEING COMMERCIALS.

WITH THE MONEY YOU PAY HIM, HE IS EITHER A BIG TIPPER BOTH WAYS OR HE NEEDS A RAISE.

EVEN A HORSE STOPS FOR WATER

SERIOUSLY

I'M REFERING TO ED McMAHON

- How many times he scratched his hands at the desk (many thought Johnny had a dry skin condition)
- How many times he put his hands in his pockets during the monologue

"I wish you would give that side kick of yours a few extra bucks. It seems to me he needs it.

Every time I turn on the TV or radio he trying to sell something. First he was selling magazine subscriptions & giving away $10 million dollars. Now he is selling life insurance. First thing you know he will be selling ["condroms"] it a big thing here in NY.

Take care of him so he can spend his late years relaxed with a few drinks instead of running from one studio to another making commercials.

With the money you pay him, he is either a big tipper both ways or he needs a raise.

Even a horse stops for water."

Look-Alikes

"My uncle looks just like Johnny!" Thousands upon thousands of viewers out there had relatives who looked just like Johnny, or so they thought. The photographs would stream in. Some did bear a resemblance, but most didn't share the slightest similarity. When the Mary Cassatt stamp was issued by the U.S. Postal Service, we received at least 50 stamps every week by people who thought there was such a striking resemblance between Johnny doing his Carnac character and Mary, that eventually Johnny did a special segment about the stamp on the show.

N.B.C. Station
Burbank, California

Mr Johnny Carson,

Dear Sir,

When you come on the stage you alway's put your hands into your pocket's, and the lining of your coat show's in the back. Now your thinking so what of it, I suppose.

I'll tell you why I'm telling you this. From the front view it look's like your shirt tail is hanging out.

May I suggest that you have the lining in your coat closer to the color of your coat, so when you stick your hand's into your pocket's the light lining doesn't show.

"When you come on the stage, you alway's put your hands into your pocket's, and the lining of your coat show's in the back. Now [your] thinking so what of it, I suppose.

I'll tell you why I'm telling you this. From the front view it look's like your shirt tail is hanging out.

May I suggest that you have the lining in your coat closer to the color of your coat, so when you stick your hands into your pocket's the light lining doesn't show.

Give this some thought Mr Carson.

I watch your show every night and enjoy it very much. And I'll watch it until you decide to retire Glad to hear you renewed your contract for another year.

God Bless.

Your's truly,

P.S. I know one should have the lining different but not for you because of craming your hands into your pocket's every show.

One would think Mr Fred De Cordava would say something to you about doing that, his right there in front of you."

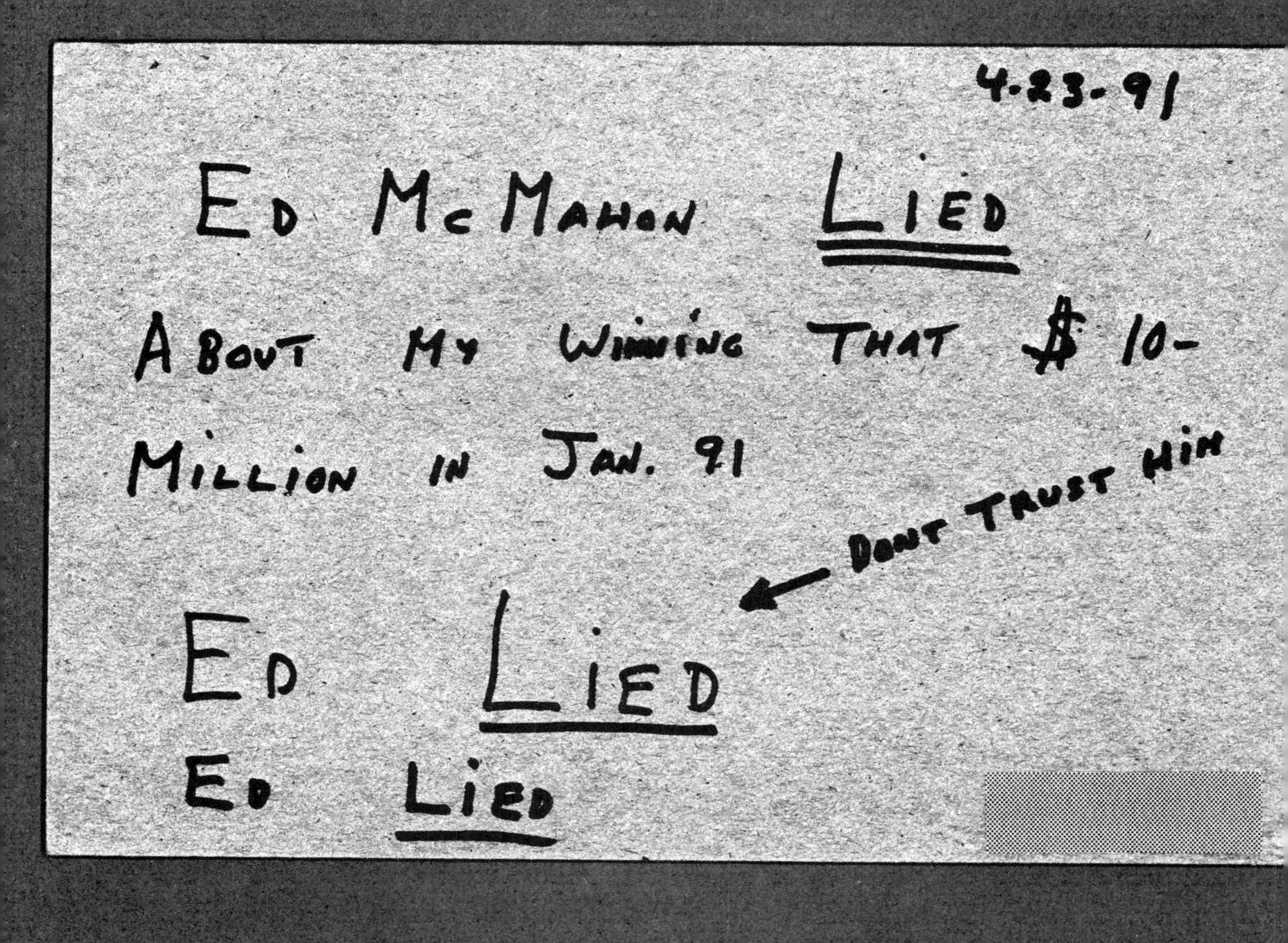
4-23-91
ED McMAHON LIED
ABOUT MY WINNING THAT $10-
MILLION IN JAN. 91
DONT TRUST HIM
ED LIED
ED LIED

Another satisfied customer.

Dear Johnny Carson: Re: THURS. SHOW

I Liked Chevy Chase's Suit. However, he was, as usual, unfunny and a bore. I think he'd make a good Serious Actor. [Seriously] why not?

The Smothers Brothers were a BORE, as usual. You should have had them tell about their DAYS AS TRAITORS. [OR ABOUT STOMPING WINE GRAPES.]

The ONLY Talent that was displayed was when Doc SEVERNSON [Just by a fluke] got to play FLIGHT of THE BUMBLE BEE ON TRUMPET. GREAT.

I didn't hear the girl singer, because I fell asleep during the Smother's Brothers Doggie CRAP.

Your Faithful critic,

P.S. When are you going to let the Tenor SAX MAN TAKE A full Solo? How ABOUT FORMING A DixieLAND BAND! Johnny, CAN YOU LAST UNTIL MAY?

But what did you *really* think about the show?

Dear Johnny Carson;

I know you don't like fruit cake? But I do, so find enclosed is the labels from Entenmann's products, which I brought and did not give to anyone else at Xmas (1991) time.

Yours truly,

FRUIT CAKE
GIFT BOX
YOU PAY
$6.99
NET WT. 24 OZ. (1 LB. 8 OZ.)
LAST SALE DATE-SEE BOX BOTTOM
PEEL TO REMOVE LABEL

FRUIT CAKE
GIFT BOX
YOU PAY
$6.99
NET WT. 24 OZ. (1 LB. 8 OZ.)
LAST SALE DATE-SEE BOX BOTTOM
PEEL TO REMOVE LABEL

FRUIT CAKE
GIFT BOX
YOU PAY
$6.99
NET WT. 24 OZ. (1 LB. 8 OZ.)
LAST SALE DATE-SEE BOX BOTTOM
PEEL TO REMOVE LABEL

FRUIT CAKE
GIFT BOX
YOU PAY
$6.99
NET WT. 24 OZ. (1 LB. 8 OZ.)
LAST SALE DATE-SEE BOX BOTTOM
PEEL TO REMOVE LABEL

FRUIT CAKE
GIFT BOX
YOU PAY
$6.99
NET WT. 24 OZ. (1 LB. 8 OZ.)
LAST SALE DATE-SEE BOX BOTTOM
PEEL TO REMOVE LABEL

FRUIT CAKE
GIFT BOX
YOU PAY
$6.99
NET WT. 24 OZ. (1 LB. 8 OZ.)
LAST SALE DATE-SEE BOX BOTTOM
PEEL TO REMOVE LABEL

"NEW & IMPROVED FLAVOR"
FRUIT CAKE
GIFT BOX
YOU PAY
$6.99
NET WT. 24 OZ. (1 LB. 8 OZ.)
LAST SALE DATE-SEE BOX BOTTOM
PEEL TO REMOVE LABEL

"NEW & IMPROVED FLAVOR"
FRUIT CAKE
GIFT BOX
YOU PAY
$6.99

FRUIT CAKE
GIFT BOX
YOU PAY
$6.99
NET WT. 24 OZ. (1 LB. 8 OZ.)
LAST SALE DATE-SEE BOX BOTTOM

Good Housekeeping magazine from December 1991 →

CITY DUMP
METAL
PERISHABLE
FRUITCAKES

Chapter Four **Who, What, and Why?**

The bulk of the mail was from individuals who needed to express themselves by either free-associating or by rambling. When we first started on the job, we wouldn't hesitate to read through every letter without much consideration to the length. We must admit however, that as the years went by, a slightly cynical and jaded attitude naturally started to develop. As soon as we read the first paragraph, we knew if we were dealing with a person who inhabited this earth or hailed from an unknown galaxy. Many letters started off quite normally, only to descend into the depths of another dimension… far, far away.

"I know you don't like fruit cake? But I do, so find enclosed is the labels from Entenmann's products, which I brought and did not give to anyone else at X'mas (1991) time.

Yours truly,

Old Fruitcake."

At least eight times a day, we would open letters at the same time, look at one another, and just say, *"Why?!"* (Why did this person send us clippings from their little boy's first haircut?) Neither one of us could ever answer because some of the mail simply surpassed explanation. When staff members would venture into our office, they would pick up an item at random,

Dear Dr. Carson,

I love you and I care for you. I hope some of my other correspondence has reached you.

I want you to stop the persecution bothering Stephanie K. in [redacted] I want you to really do something about it. She is my sister and I think you know what is going on here to some degree. She is a wonderful sister and you have to really help her, you have to do something for her.

look at one of us, and ask, *"Why?!... Why did this person send you their toilet seat?"* Our response was merely, *"Here's their address. You find out!"*

"Dear Dr. Carson,

I love you and I care for you. I hope some of my other correspondence has reached you.

I want you to stop the persecution bothering Stephanie K. in [ ]. I want you to really do something about it. She is my sister and I think you know what is going on here to some degree. She is a wonderful sister and you have to really help her. You have to do something for her.

There is so much to appreciate about her that I have to tell you. You seem so wonderful and you know so many people. Help her.

Tell Alan King to help her. Tell Paul [Riser] to help her. I really want her to get some encouragement.

I need a job playing with your band. give me a job. Can you offer me that?

Do contact me if you have the energy. I love you.

Praise God,
[ ] - Christ"

After opening this kind of mail through the years, we were proud of the fact that *nothing* could faze us. We were immune to surprise, shock, and "gross-out" (although we must admit, when we received the letter containing toenail clippings, a muted scream came from our office; but aside from that, we were solid as rocks).

All right I'll swallow it.

Oh No! Oh No!

If we were unable to stay for the taping at 5:30 p.m., we would catch the show later that evening. We'd cringe whenever Johnny mentioned something on the air that we knew would generate tons and tons of mail. From time to time, we both fantasized that Johnny would announce that everyone should stop writing letters for at least a week!

The Grossest Things We Opened

While we opened our share of soiled letters stained with unknown substances and sauces, the three strangest and most appalling items we encountered were the used toilet paper, the aforementioned toenail clippings, and the (by now, several weeks old) homemade stewed tomatoes sent in a leaky plastic container. We were convinced someone had shipped us their gall bladder.

"All right, I'll swallow it."

The shortest letter received; straight to the point, but what are they swallowing?

July

Dear Johnnie,

I usually would write to my brother today but he's not at home. He lives in California and now is visiting his Grandma in Minnesota. I'm proud of him but don't understand him as I don't understand you. (I'm smiling), are you crying. (I'm sorry) I love you!

a Fair and Camping that coming up and I hope I don't have to go. I scared of guns and another thing, Pictures and undressed people. Please help me and find a way I can stay at home. Please.

"I usually would write to my brother [ ] today but he's not at home. He lives in California and now is visiting his Grandma in Minnesota. I'm proud of him but don't understand him as I don't understand you. (I'm smiling), are you crying. (I'm sorry) I love you!

A [Fair] and [camping] that coming up and I hope I don't have to go. I scared of guns and another thing, pictures and undressed people. Please help me and find a way I can stay at home. Please.

I'm sorry for what I said help [ ] and yourself

Can I tell you some thing I hear. Remember what happen between Terry and Tony – but why did they keep saying - keep your eyes set infront of you and don't look out these windows like you and boys said to me afraid of my picture taken? Why? I love those birds and squirell. I told farmers to stop using guns to kill black birds and use square man. I hear last year they really went out in farmer's yard.

I love you very much!"

JOHNNY CARSON
THE LATE SHOW
LOS ANGELES, CALIF.
U.S.A.

HOPE YOU ARE NOT TOO OFFENDED, BUT I AM SENDING MY TOE NAIL CUTTINGS, WHICH USUALLY ARE FLUSHED DOWN THE TOILE.

THIS IS THE MEASURE OF HUMAN (OR ANYONE SET UPON SOMETHING) SACRIFICE THAT I GO ALONG WITH UNDER DURESS.

YOU HAVE THE OPPORTUNITY TO DISPLAY TO YOUR SHARKIES, IN YOURSCABNATION, HOW MUCH ENTITLEMENT THEY HAVE (ZERO, IDEALLY) TO OTHER PRIVATE LIVES (PARDON THE PSYCHO).

SINCERELY.

P.S. DISRUPTION LIMITED.

"Hope you are not too offended, but I am sending my toe nail cuttings, which usually are flushed down the [toile].

This is the measure of human (anyone set upon or something) sacrifice that I go along with under duress.

You have the opportunity to display to your sharkies, in your scabnation[?], how much entitlement they have (zero ideally) to other private lives (pardon the psycho).

P.S. Disruption limited."

This letter generated the most groans of any correspondence ever received by our office, bar none!

1979 NEB.
Children
PM
27 JAN
1987
Sinclair Lewis
USA 14
Abraham Baldwin
USA 7
USA 22
Reticulated Helmet
Johnny Carson
The Tonight Show
N.B.C. Studios
Burbank, Calif.
U.S.A.

Ah… the minimalist. This envelope contained five pages free of any written words. Did they forget to write or can we just fill in the blanks?

is written, he ...
...om a child (youth) shall have him become his son

4497. מָנוֹן mânôwn, maw-nohn'; from ... continuator, i.e. heir:—son.

...t is, his heir) at the length

319. אַחֲרִית 'achărîyth, akh-ar-eeth'; from 310; the last or end, hence the future; also posterity:—(last, latter) end (time), hinder (utter) -most, length, posterity, remnant, residue, reward.

(This is in the pa... of the Jewish lang... the Patriarc...

...in the Greek:

...w I say, that the heir

2818. κληρονόμος klērŏnŏmŏs, klay-ron-om'-os; from 2819 and the base of 3551 (in its orig. sense of partitioning, i.e. [reflex.] getting by apportionment); a sharer by lot, i.e. an inheritor (lit. or fig.); by impl. a possessor:—heir.

3551 (law)

(that is, the hei...

...ording to the law), as long as he is a child

3516. νήπιος nēpiŏs, nay'-pee-os; from a... particle νη- nē- (implying negation) and ... speaking, i.e. an infant (minor); fig. a simple-person, an immature Christian:—babe, child

...ek defin. 3551 is the law the Greek and comes from the Jewish language of the Patriarchs which is the Penteteuch)

...fereth nothing from a bondservant, though he be lord of ...

...is under tutors

2012. ἐπίτροπος ĕpitrŏpŏs, ep-it'-rop-os; from 1909 and 5158 (in the sense of 2011); a commissioner, i.e. domestic manager, guardian:—steward, tutor.

, and governors

3623. οἰκονόμος ŏikŏnŏmŏs, ... from 3624 and the base of 3551; a ho... (i.e. manager), or overseer, i.e. an em... capacity; by extens. a fiscal agent (tr... preachers (of the Gospel):—chamberl... steward.

...is, preachers of the Gospel) until the time appointed

4287. προθέσμιος prŏthĕsmiŏs, proth-es'-mee-os; from 4253 and a der. of 5087; fixed beforehand, i.e. (fem. with 2250 impl.) a designated day:—time appointed.

...e Father.

...in, whoso looketh into the perfect

5046. τέλειος tĕlĕiŏs, tel'-i-os; from 5056; complete (in various applications of labor, growth, mental and moral character, etc.); neut. (as noun, with 3588) completeness:—of full age, man, perfect.

...w

3551. νόμος nŏmŏs, nom'-os; from a prim. νέμω nĕmō (to parcel out, espec. food or grazing to animals); law (through the idea of prescriptive usage), gen. (regulation), spec. (of Moses [includ. the volume]; also of the Gospel), or fig. (a principle):—law.

of LIBERTY

1657. ἐλευθερία ĕlĕuthĕria, el-yoo-ther-ee'-ah; from 1658; freedom (legitimate or licentious, chiefly mor. or cer.):—liberty.

1658. ἐλεύθερος ĕlĕuthĕrŏs, el-yoo'-ther-os; prob. from the alt. of 2064; unrestrained (to go at pleasure), i.e. (as a citizen) not a slave (whether freeborn or manumitted), or (gen.) exempt (from obligation or liability):—free (man, woman), at liberty.

1659. ἐλευθερόω ĕlĕuthĕrŏō, el-yoo-ther-ŏ'-o; from 1658; to liberate, i.e. (fig.) to exempt (from mor., cer. or mortal liability):—deliver, make free.

ἐλεύθω ĕlĕuthō. See 2064.

(This is Greek for LAW which is justice (especially divine law) and not what this world calls the laws for legal injustice is not justice) which you will learn.

...d continueth therein, he being not a forgetful hearer, b...

...doer

4163. ποιητής pŏiētēs, poy-ay-tace'; from 4160; a performer; spec. a "poet":—doer, poet.

of the work

2041. ἔργον ĕrgŏn, er'-gon; from a prim. (but obsol.) ἔργω ĕrgō (to work); toil (as an effort or occupation); by impl. an act:—deed, doing, labour, work.

2040. ἐργάτης ĕrgatēs, er... a toiler; fig. a teacher:—labour...

...s man shall be blessed

3107. μακάριος makariŏs, mak-ar'-ee-os; a prol. form of the poetical μάκαρ makar (mean. the same); supremely blest; by extens. fortunate, well off:—blessed, happy (× -ier).

in his

...ed

4162. ποίησις pŏiēsis, poy'-ay-sis; from 4160; action, i.e. performance (of the law):—deed.

...in, Speak not evil one of another, brethren. He that speak...

...l of his brother

80. ἀδελφός adĕlphŏs, ad-el-fos'; from 1 (as a connective particle) and δελφύς dĕlphus (the womb); a brother (lit. or fig.) near or remote ...

79. ἀδελφή adĕlphē, ad-el-fay'; fem. of 80; a sister (nat. or eccles.):—sister

, an...

This is only a portion of a 20-foot long letter that was taped together and mailed in a large cardboard cracker box.

MR. JOHNNY CARSON.

DEAR MR. CARSON I HAVE LEFT OR RAN AWAY FROM THE CATHOLIC CHURCH ABOUT THIRTY YEARS AGO, AND I'M GLAD I DID IT.

THE OTHER DAY THE CATHOLICS WERE CELEBRATING THEIR USUAL ASH WEDNSDAY, BY PLACING ASHES OVER THE FOREHEADS OF THEIR FOLLOWERS.

I HAVE ABOUT THREE OR FOUR CONCORDANCES ON HOW TO FIND ANYTHING IN THE BIBLE.

ASH WEDNESDAY IS NOT ANYWHERE IN THE BIBLE.

IF I CAN REMEMBER CORRECTLY WHEN THE PRIEST PLACES THE ASHES ON THE FOREHEADS OF THE PARISHIONERS , HE SAYS OR MUMBLES (FROM DUST THOU ART AND TO DUST SHALT THOU RETURN.)

AND THESE WORDS THAT THE PRIEST MUTTERS ARE IN A SECTION OF THE BIBLE THAT THE CATHOLIC CHURCH REFERS TO AS A MYTH. I HAVE A COPY OF A BULLETIN WHICH SAYS THAT THE FIRST ELEVEN CHAPTERS OF THE BIBLE ARE A MYTH.

YET THIS SAME HYPOCRYTICAL CHURCH COMES ALONG WITH THEIR ASH WEDNESDAY BIT AND USES THE WORDS THAT ARE ONLY FOUND IN THE THIRD CHAPTER OF GENESIS AT VERSE NINETEEN, THE VERY SECTION WHICH THE CATHOLIC CHURCH CALLS A MYTH. THAT IN ANY MANS LANGUAGE IS HYPOCRYTICAL.

GOD SAYS FOR PEOPLE LIKE THAT TO EITHER MAKE IT OR GET OFF THE POT.

INDEED THE CATHOLIC CHURCH IS NOT A CHURCH AT ALL , BUT A BIG POLITICAL ORGANIZATION WITH RELIGION AS A FRONT AND THEY DON'T BELIEVE IN ONE BIT OF WHAT GOD SAYS IN HIS BIBLE.

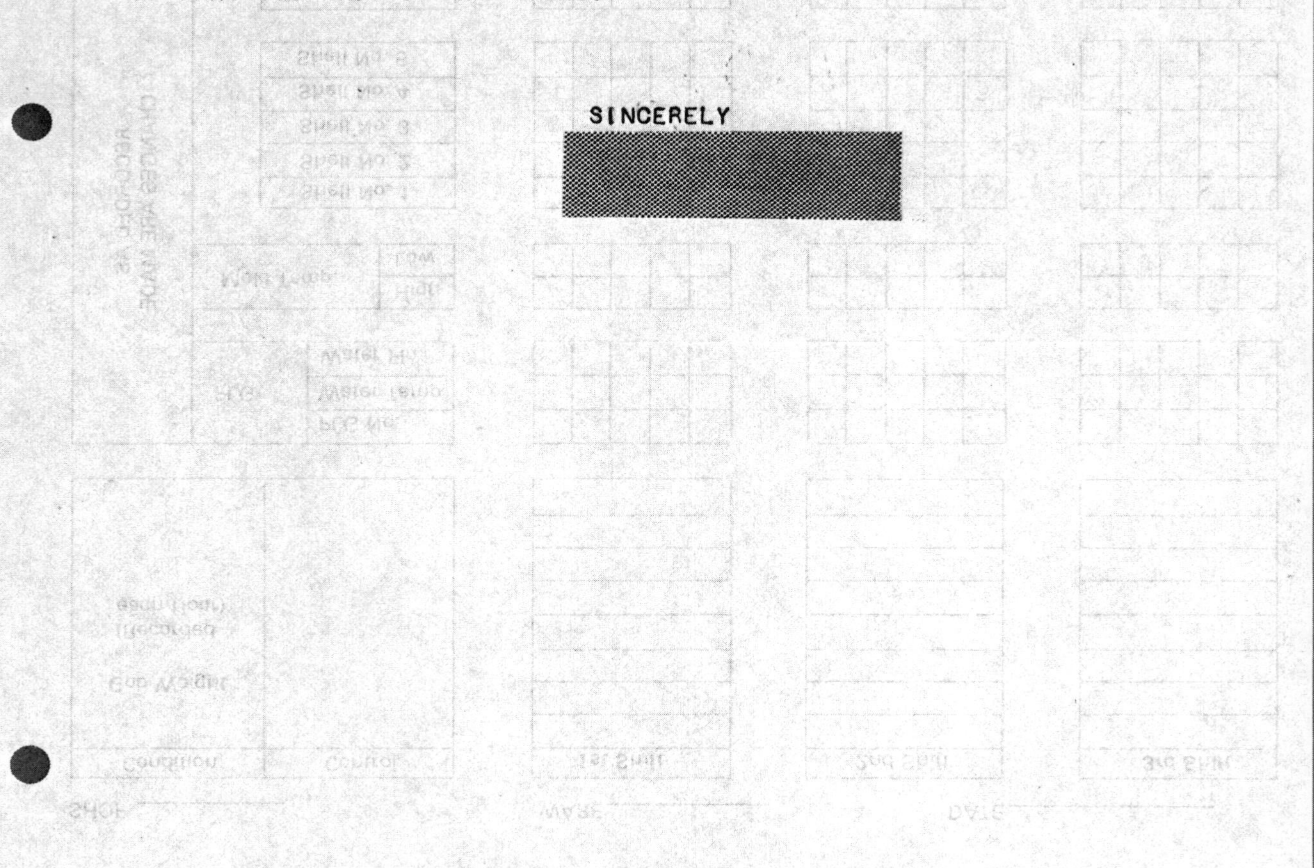

SINCERELY

When people got angry about *anything,* they vented to Johnny.

Mr. Johnny Carson
"The Tonight Show"
NBC-TV
Burbank, California 91523

CERTIFIED MAIL

Dear Johnny:

Re: Program on November 7 --

You will remember that on Oct. 24 I wrote to you, enclosing a $50 bill because of your good work in helping Mr. Mondale to get elected. I am enclosing another $50 bill and a copy of my previous letter in case you didn't see it (or the first $50).

I was glad to see tonight that you are true to your own self and just as funny, clever and entertaining as ever, because I worry about you.

I just about died laughing at your jokes about Ronnie, and thought it was real sweet of you to make such a nice serious speech complimenting Mr. Mondale on his gracious and classy talk conceding the election.

I thought Ronnie's acceptance speech was the "pits," didn't you? I thought sure you would mention it. I don't think he should have been so happy. Who voted for him anyhow?...a bunch of nitwits. (53,428,357)

I felt sorry for you and worried when your audience "booed" your joke about Nancy holding a sign over Maureen's head saying "This one isn't mine." I can't see why they booed. I suppose they thought Maureen might feel terribly hurt -- or that it might make Maureen and Nancy sick, and Ronnie too. They don't know like I do -- that you would never do anything to really hurt one's feelings. So what -- you rip up a family. They're still alive.

I hope being booed hasn't made you sick. I worry about you.

My neighbor over the back fence thinks you're sadistic and mean and un-Americqn. She has the crazy idea that by ridiculing and showing such a lack of respect for people in public office (especially the President), that you are doing our country a great disservice. She thinks Ronnie is the greatest president we have ever had and a wonderful man, who is really too good for the milieu. We argue about it -- I don't think you're a liberal leftist, demeaning our country and ridiculing anything or anybody that is conservative, moral, or decent. We argue about it; I hate it when people criticise you, because I worry about you.

So even if election is over, I still want to send you another $50, I'll see you in my dreams.

Lots of love,

Enc.-One $50 bill.

cc: Fred de Cordova
Ed McMahon
President Reagan
NBC-TV (Robt. Mulholland. Pres.)
✓ NBC-TV (Burbank)

P.S. Are you still happy with your latest whats-her-name -- Alex or Axle or something? BOY-does she have a "built."! Or do the young call it something else - maybe like what Bush said ? ?

Political ramblings made up a large percentage of the mail. By the way, we never got the $50.00.

In this white room with white typing paper and white thesaurus is something called a scatter brain. Similar to the shark brain, the scatter brain will attempt to devour everything in sight. One problem here: for the shark it is called instinct....for the scatter brain, it is called civilized....HO. HO..HA..HA..AIIIII....and of the two, the scatter is supposed to be the most adventurous and by far the most dangerous.....

...chug, chug, chug a lug...as the roller coaster slipping and sliding tried to accelerate, but the towering incline made speed an impossibility..... and everyone raised their hands at the near ascension to the top.....and then braced for the exploding downhill launch of the ten-car projectile..... as all are thrown backwards.....they scream aie... aieeeee.....aieeeeeee.....

Dealing with humans is unpredictable and usually relegated to superficial artificiality. The paradox of chaos versus order demonstrated nothing...for cruel was easy, but stepping into the real world was very tricky for the painfully shy figure from the sylvan. What was that stupid adage...never let them see you sweat....Ha. Ha. Ha....the knees crumbled, the smile vanished, the mouth became dry and the pompous cackled...." Dont Sweat!" Win some...lose some... but the wins never make up for all the losses...

Free association?

Johnny Carson
c/o The Tonight Show
NBC-TV Studios
Hollywood, California

Dear Johnny,

If I were a standup comic doing a guest shot on your show for the first time, I'd look at the audience for a slightly prolonged period, then turn to you, and ask, "where's the men's room?" I would then go into my routine accompanied by the sound of water running for a breif period. I might even let the water run every time a joke bombed; however, I'm not connected to the entertainment world in any way, and I prefer to remain so, but the above is one of my rare quirks, and I wonder about audience reaction.

Many years ago, when I lived in Manhattan, I went into my neighborhood apothecary to buy a jar of glycerine suppositories. This was not the usual type of drug stores, but strictly a supplier of health care items, and the men were formally attired, like you, and appeared to be very dignified. As I looked at the jar of suppositories, I uttered with a straight face, "I hope this will be enough; I'm throwing a party." The druggist struggled to hold back a smile, and continued to do so for some time whenever I entered the store, and I marvel at the durability of such a simple joke. I'm strange. I laugh when I hear genuine laughter without hearing the joke. sometimes I try to provoke laughter with or without a straight face, and I occasionally come up spontaneously not realizing how much more humorous I am without trying. Be that as it may, I enjoy the feeling I get from it. If you decide to try the standup comic bit, to test audience reaction, please do not mention my name; I don't want any publicity. If you feel that you must drop a name, please make it Cecil Poole; "Cess" for short.

I don't want to waste paper, so here's a spoof on tabloids for your personal amusement:

Jean-Luc Piccard, captain of the Fedration Starship, U.S.S. Enterprise, and his crew discover three cube shaped sister planets, each respectively inhabited by Croutons, Bouillons, and Cubans.

I'm not a bigot (I tell people my YUGO is a Polish Ferrari), but some Cubans might be offended. I should think that the only resemblence to earthbound Cubans would be space ships that are shaped like cigars.

Respectfully,

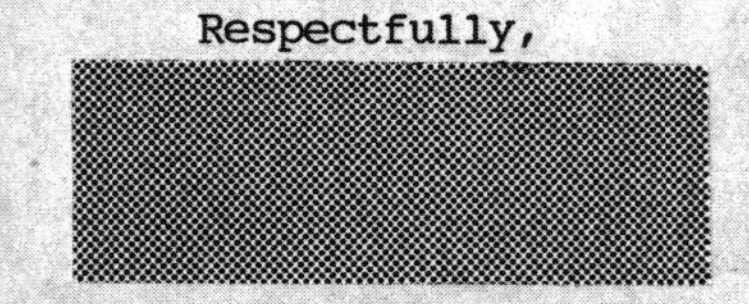

This is an example of a well-constructed letter from an obviously bright person. Unfortunately, his letter just didn't make any sense to us. Then again, it could have been written by an aspiring comic (being clever?) wanting to make his debut on the "Tonight Show." Many viewers just wanted to be discovered.

Dear Johnny Carson

Before you leave us in May (a black time for us avid fans), please settle an argument:

Are the (4) buttons on your suit jackets made special in the material of rhinestone or other stone? They pick up the light and are so attractive when you do your monologue.

Please advise and thanks (in advance) for your trouble

Sincerely Yours

Chapter Five Questions, Questions, Questions

We must admit, it was exceedingly difficult to answer some of the questions that viewers would pose to Johnny in their letters. We were more than happy to respond to those queries that applied specifically to the "Tonight Show." Folks usually just wanted to know what year the show first aired, what guests were going to be appearing, how to secure tickets, how to find a product that Johnny spoke of on the show, who that lady with the curly hair who sang the song by the piano two nights ago was, or maybe how to get their tap-dancing senior citizen group on the program.

"Before you leave us in May (a bleak time for us avid fans), please settle an argument:

Are the (4) buttons on your suit jackets made special in the material of rhinestone or other stone? They pick up the light and are so attractive when you do your monologue.

Please advise and thanks (in advance) for your trouble."

Then there were "those" questions. The questions that were abstract, askew and perplexing. Although we rarely missed a taping in all our years with the show, we never noticed the details that some of our eagle-eyed viewers observed; such as, *"Why does Johnny always wear sportcoats and never a suit?"*

Dear Mr. Carson

I watch the Tonight Show all the time and I will be sad when you leave the show. I enjoy the show very Mutch. However there is one thing that have puzzled me for some time, that is how the Tonight Show theam song is being played by the band as you are being intruduced

I notice that the theam song is played different when Tommy Newsom leads the band, than when "Doc". Severson leads the band. When Tommy leads the band, at the end of the song when the band plays that "Dot da-da-da-da—Dot Dot". the band Cuts off one measure of the song. When "Doc". leads the band the band Continues for a nother measure. Please explain to me why they do this

Thank You

Big Question

A common question people continued to ask over the years was, *"Why is the curtain that Johnny stands in front of striped and the curtain the guest host stands in front of grey/blue?"* Answer: the "Star" got the "stripes."

"I watch the Tonight Show all the time and I will be sad when you leave the show. I enjoy the show very [mutch]. However, there is one thing that has puzzled me for sometime, that is how the Tonight Show theme song is being played by the band as you are being introduced.

I notice that the theme song is played different when Tommy Newsom leads the band, than when "Doc" [Severson] leads the band. When Tommy leads the band, at the end of the song when the band plays that "Dot da-da-da-da-Dot Dot" the band cuts off one measure of the song. When "Doc" leads the band the band continues for another measure.

Please explain to me why they do this.

Thank You."

Dear Mr. Carson,

Noticed a picture of you with your parents in the PEOPLE magazine of 19 August 91, page 77.

Are your mother's shoes on the opposite foot? Sure looks like it to me. My podiatrist says it may be an optical illusion. But the nurse and receptionist agreed with me that the shoes are on wrong. Well—?

Hope to receive a reply. Thanks.

Sincerely,

"Noticed a picture of you with your parents in the People magazine of 19 August 91. page 77.

Are your mother's shoes on the opposite foot? Sure looks like it to me. My podiatrist says it may be an optical illusion. But the nurse and receptionist agreed with me that the shoes are on wrong. Well... ?

Hope to receive a reply. Thanks."

Mr Johnny Carson

Dear Mr. Carson:

I have watched your show from its beginning 29 years ago until the present time.

On occasion you pass out cards for your audience to ask questions which you usually answer rather facetiously.

I have two questions which I think many viewers would like to hear your answers.

(1) Is there an unwritten law in California that outlaws suits - that is 2 pieces - Jackets and Trousers to be the same color and of the same material, rather than a jacket of one suit with the trousers of another?

(2) Why do these so-called song writers and singers, guitar players need long unkempt hair, and wear "Salvation army rejects" clothing (as per enclosed picture.

"I have watched your show from its beginning 29 years ago until the present time.

On occasion you pass out cards for your audience to ask questions which you usually answer rather facetiously.

I have two questions which I think many viewers would like to hear your answers.

(1) Is there an unwritten law in California that outlaw's suits that is 2 pieces - Jackets and Trousers to be the same color and of the same material, rather then a jacket of one suit with the trousers of another?

(2) Why do these so called song-writers and singers, guitar players need long unkempt hair and wear "Salvation Army reject" clothing (as per enclosed picture.)

I'll be sorry to see you retire from your show - but I'll agree that 30 years of doing the same thing tends to become tiresome."

March 5, 1992

Dear Johnny,

Why are all of your striped ties left handed as opposed to right handed??

LEFT

RIGHT

WE WILL MISS YOU!!

Old Friends,

Good question.
Are there any more good questions?

N B C Studios
3000 W. Alamenda Avenue
Burbank, California 91523

ATT: TONIGHT SHOW - Mr. Johnny Carson

Dear Johnny -

I have watched "The Tonight Show" for many years with delight! However, as an ophthalmologist, I have wondered how you have managed to read small print from newspaper clippings etc. without glasses. Are you myopic? (near-sighted) Do you wear contact lenses? Have you had refractive surgery? Does your staff cue in large print for you? May I even ask you these questions?

Thank you for years of laughter!!

Sincerely,

Yes, you may ask all those questions. But no, we can't always answer them.

Johnny Carson
C/O The Tonight show
Burbank, California

Dear Johnny,

I have been watching the Tonight Show most of my life, and I'm 71 years old. I've had some questions and suggestions for you for a long long time, and now, I just could not let you leave without writing this letter. Hope it's not to late. Ready or not, here goes:

1. When most of your guests come out (especially the men - but not always) they shake hands with you, then they go up to Ed and take <u>both</u> of their hands and shake Ed's. Why is that? And, if you don't believe this, check back far as you like.

2. When you come out on the stage, there is a colorful curtain behind you. When Jay Leno comes out, the curtain is a dull grey. Why is that?

3. Too late for this one (I should have written 30 years ago). Many times you talk to the audience, the audience talks back, but we don't hear them! Thus, we miss out on some jokes that way. Why was that?

4. (Optional) Johnny, some times it seems to me that you lisp. Is it my ears or you?

5. And, for 30 years now Ed has been saying, "Hereeeeeeeers Johnny". How about just till May 22 having Ed say, "Ladies and gentlemen, here's Johnny." It would be a refreshing change.

I love you,

We appreciate your questions but… maybe it's time for you to get involved in your local community.

Dear Mr. Carson,

I am appalled by the "cheap shot" you made last week regarding the restoration of Lawrence Welk's house. This joke could only have been written by an ignoramus and I am shocked that you would repeat it over national television.

It is so easy to take "cheap shots" at Mr. Welk who is now in his late 80's and in frail health.

It seems to me that you should get your facts straight regarding the restoration of the Welk house. They are restoring it, not specifically because it is Mr. Welk's house, but because it is an example of pioneer life on the prairie in North Dakota. He just happens to be the most famous member of the ethnic group—

(1-

Not a joke, a word, a gesture or a look from Johnny while on the air, went by our keen viewers without a comment or criticism. We received constant complaints about the political jokes in the monologue, and believe it or not, grievances about the number of times Johnny licked his fingers while turning pages or when he straightened his tie.

"I am appalled by the "cheap shot" you made last week regarding the restoration of Lawrence Welk's house. This joke could only have been written by an ignoramus and I am shocked that you would repeat it over national television.

It is so easy to take "cheap shots" at Mr. Welk who is now in his late 80's and in frail health.

It seems to me that you should get your facts straight regarding the restoration of the Welk house. They are restoring it, not specifically because it is Mr. Welk's house, but because it is an example of pioneer life on the prairie in North Dakota. He just happens to be the most famous member of the ethnic group – "

Yes, viewers actually took the time and the trouble to count his licking and his straightening and then would write to him to let him know the results of their research. We often wondered why these folks couldn't take that same energy to write to their congressman about some serious and pressing issues instead of worrying about Johnny's personal habits.

Mr. Carson,

I heard you thank Buddy Hackett the other night for appearing on your show for "poverty wages". I think this was an insensitive remarkand shows how out of touch high paid personalities can be. Most of the people in our area don't make in a week those poverty wages that your guests make as scale pay for a few minutes' appearance.

Sincerely,

While the majority thought Johnny was fantastic working with animals, there were always those who felt he was poking fun at them every time the audience laughed during an animal segment. We remember a flood of mail after we had a parrot on the program that just refused to speak. The segment was hysterical because Johnny held up the rubber chicken that was kept behind his desk, looked at the parrot and said, "This is what happened to the last non-talking bird we had on the show!" The audience roared, but the next day, letters poured in from parrot activist groups (we're not kidding) accusing Johnny of cruelty because they thought he had threatened the parrot's life.

"I heard you thank Buddy Hackett the other night for appearing on your show for "poverty wages." I think this was an insensitive remark and shows how out of touch high paid personalities can be. Most of the people in our area don't make in a week those poverty wages that your guests make as scale pay for a few minutes' appearance."

For four years we responded to viewers who were livid about the constant jokes Johnny (and everyone else) made about Dan Quayle. While everyone has a right to be P.O'd at times, we sometimes wondered if those who complained the most understood that the "Tonight Show" was a comedy program.

N.B.C
The Tonight Show
51 West 52nd
N.Y. N.Y. 10019

Mr. Carson

Watched your show, [redacted] You + Chuby Chase have your nerve criticizing the hosts of the Olimpecs. I can picture you doing it with out jokes to pull you through. Chuby Chase was as interesting as that fellow who talked about herbs. Remember him? And by the way what the hell do you have aganist Dudley Moore. You treated him like wallpaper.

Sincerely
[redacted]

Fans Hated The Form Letter

Unfortunately, due to the enormous quantity of mail we received, it was impossible to answer each letter personally. We were therefore relegated to send out the dreaded FORM LETTER! We had a form letter on just about every subject. Understandably, viewers loathed these impersonal responses and would become terribly irate upon receipt of one.

"Watched your show, [ ]. You & [Chuby] Chase have your nerve criticizing the hosts of the [Olimpics]. I can picture you doing it with out jokes to pull you through.

[Chuby] Chase was as interesting as that fellow who talked about herbs. Remember him? And by the way what the hell do you have [aganist] Dudley Moore. You treated him like wallpaper."

Some of the form letters we sent out were:

- Thank you for writing
- Thank you for the gift
- Thank you for the poem
- Thank you for the card
- Thank you for the book
- Thank you for the idea
- Thank you for the talent suggestion
- Thank you for the talent information
- Our policy for musical acts
- We can't offer you advice
- We can't participate in your project

Dear Mr Carson.

I'm a viewer from way back, and thought you were always a snappy dresser.

But alas, as of late you seem to become a real professor looking host.

Leave the fall colours behind, and get back to the blues, grays, black and lighter shades. The browns and tweeds does not become you.

Still think you are the best of all the interviewers on TV.

Sincerely

- Sorry to hear of your displeasure
- Sorry Johnny can't attend your graduation
- With regrets, we must turn down your invitation
- With regrets, we cannot send you money
- Thank you for the children's material
- Sorry we're sending back your written material
- We're unable to fulfill your request

"I'm a viewer from way back, and thought you were always a snappy dresser.

But alas, as of late you seem to become a real professor looking host.

Leave the fall colours behind, and get back to the blues, grays, black and lighter shades. The browns and tweeds does not become you.

Still think you are the best of all the interviewers on TV."

12:31 A.M.

Dear Mr. Carson,

I have just finished viewing your most enjoyable show with Dudley More, et al.

The music was great and the Comedian very funny; however, I cannot stand the noise the microphones pick up when you thump on your desk. It also happens when Jay Leno is the guest host, but his "thumps" are even louder. I have a notion that your desk is very light weight (cheap) & that is why we are bothered with this terrible thumping sound. Can't you do some-thing about this?

I love you, your program, & you will be greatly missed

Sincerely

"I have just finished viewing your most enjoyable show with Dudley Moore, et al.

The music was great and the comedian very funny; however, I cannot stand the noise the microphones pick up when you thump on your desk.

It also happens when Jay Leno is the guest host, but his "thumps" are even louder. I have a notion that your desk is very light weight (cheap) & that is why we are bothered with this terrible thumping sound. Can't you do something about this?

I love you, your program, & you will be greatly missed."

Mr. Johnny Carson
NBC TV
Burbank, CA

Dear Johnny:

I have watched your show for many years and always enjoyed it and you......HOWEVER, I was appalled last night when you (supposedly "joking") started viciously attacking CATS!

You are supposed to be from the farms of Nebraska so I would think you would love animals. Evidently not the case.

In this mean world where people spend money and volunteer their time and efforts to rescuing poor abused and unwanted animals I think the way you put down cats was very cruel.

With all the power you have to reach millions of people I think you could better spend your air time HELPING animals instead of encouraging people to not like them.

Cats are wonderful!!! I have had dogs and cats both and I love cats the best. They are beautiful and gentle and each has a different personality. I always marvel at their beauty and their wonderful intelligence and alertness.

In the future PLEASE try to help animals with your mouth instead of hurting them.

Sincerely,

Animal admirers complained most often. We had hundreds of letters from cat-lovers over the years. Johnny didn't hide the fact that he wasn't crazy about cats.

Johnny Carson
The Tonight Show
NBC-TV
Burbank, California

Dear Johnny,

Having watched you on television ever since "Who do you Trust", I feel I know you well enough to ask a favor. Would you, just once before you retire, properly pronounce the word AWARE? For all these years I've heard you say AWHERE---and I'll be damned if I can figure where you picked up that "H"!

Thank you for this very minor request--and as you've no doubt figured out, it doesn't take too much to make some of us happy.

Have a great retirement---you deserve it.

Sincerely,

People were always correcting Johnny's English, pronunciation, *and* diction.

Dear Johnny,

I'm disappointed!!!

I have been an avid fan of yours since the late 50's, and will be lost when you retire from the Tonight show.

The reason for my disappointment was your not appearing on your scheduled T.V. show, when the heavy rains came.

I was sitting in my living room with my son when I heard you cancelled. My son who lives in Malibu on [redacted] (right near you) had come in a few hours earlier in the rain to my home in VAN NUYS, which as you know is quite close to the N.B.C studios in Burbank

He had no mishap and was driving a car much older and I'm sure less safe than any mode of transportation you could have conjured up.

It made me feel like you were robbing your fans of an opportunity to enjoy your show because you chickened out.

I know you could have made it

Any way I forgive you. The best of luck

Sincerly, an ever loving fan

"I'm disappointed!!!

I have been an avid fan of yours since the late 50's, and will be lost when you retire from the Tonight Show.

The reason for my disappointment was you're not appearing on your scheduled T.V. show, when the heavy rains came.

I was sitting in my living room with my son when I hear you cancelled. My son who lives in Malibu on [ ] (right near you) had come in a few hours earlier, in the rain, to my home in Van Nuys, which, as you know, is quite close to the N.B.C. studios in Burbank.

He had no mishap and was driving a car much older and I'm sure less safe than any mode of transportation you could have conjured up.

It made me feel like you were robbing your fans of an opportunity to enjoy your show because you chickened out.

I know you could have made it. Any way I forgive you. The best of luck.

Sincerely, an ever loving fan."

We guess viewers had a right to think Johnny was in the same category as the U.S. Postal service... neither rain, nor snow, nor mud slide in Malibu.

FROM : P01

Mr. Johnny Carson
c/o NBC Productions
30 Rockefeller Plaza
New York, New York 10112-0001

Dear Mr. Carson:

You did a major injustice last evening when you insulted a man about whom you know little or nothing in the midst of an electoral process. You told a joke last evening in which Paul Tsongas was represented as one who could not win the presidential race. You then said you know little or nothing about the man. This is a major wrong. I insist that there is redress. I insist that you stop seeking to destroy this man's character when you have nothing upon which to base your action. If there is not some action taken on the Monday show to redress this wrong directed eventually at the hardworking American public, there may be action such as a boycott of your show and other NBC programs. I am not an official member of the Tsongas campaign, yet as an individual I should wage a national boycott due to this injustice. Good day, sir.

Thank you,

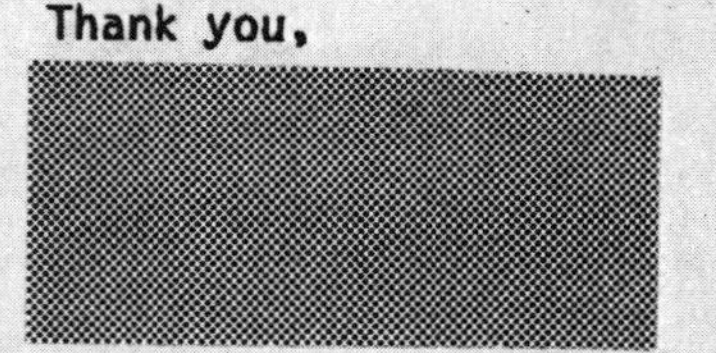

It was hard for people to understand that the monologue was a series of jokes about the day's events. It was difficult to please everyone and the next letter might be from a viewer who loved the Tsongas joke.

To Johnny Carson:
Just something from a fan.

You and Jay Leno have made constant remarks about our Vice President Quale.. He is a clean educated man that was a lawyer. He has to have orders from President Bush to do certain things.. At that time his wife was dealing with her Mother dying of breast cancer.

Nothing wrong about the National Guard. My nephews spent 8 and 11 years in it. I think it was very degrading on what was said. I am not a Republican.

So could you before you retire have some compassion and a small word of apology to him? I don't feel it is humor.

Thank you for listening and good luck.

We had numerous irate letters from Dan Quayle followers. Folks admired the then-VP, but could rarely spell his name.

Dear Johnny,

We enjoyed your anniversary show and were sorry to note your cold. However, don't you realise that if you would stop that annoying habit of licking your thumb to turn pages or cards that you would not ingest germs into your system?

How about two resolutions before you quit work: 1) stop licking your thumb and 2) more Carnack and other disguises.

A Fan

A number of fans were terribly annoyed at Johnny's finger-licking and thumping.

Johny Carson
NBC 3000 West Alameda Ave.
Burbank, CA 91505

Dear Johny:

How could you be so tactless and elicit Elizabeth Taylor's condemnation of people who write books on bedding stars and celebrities many years before, while your next guest was Michael Douglas, whose father wrote precisely that kind of book just a while ago?

A rather difficult task trying to please nearly 20 million viewers every night.

(1)

(3)

(2)

Dear Johnny,

My is [redacted] from [redacted]

Johnny knows who I am please show this letter to Johnny immediately. Call Nancy Reagan. If you have a plan to send a lawyer to my house directly they have a plan to stop him. They will lie & use any excuse so they won't be sued. I need F. Lee Bailey & Air Force 1 to get me out of this town. This doctor & FBI agent have lied & used every excuse to stop me 8 times from getting my freedom. If Nancy has sent a secret service man to protect me & fly to Switzerland the doctor convinced him to leave & told him I was getting a divorce & it was my attitude. No one in this town is to be trusted. You have to send them directly to my house. This doctor has nothing to

Chapter Seven **On the Edge**

Appearing on television is almost a guarantee that you will receive mail from every conceivable segment of society. While a percentage of the mail was from

"My [name] is [   ] from [   ]. Johnny knows who I am please show this letter to Johnny immediately. Call Nancy Reagan. If you have a plan to send a lawyer to my house directly they have a plan to stop him. They will lie & use any excuse so they won't be sued. I need F. Lee Bailey & Air Force 1 to get me out of this town. This doctor & FBI agent have lied & used every excuse to stop me 8 times from getting my freedom. If Nancy has sent a secret service man to protect me & fly to Switzerland the doctor convinced him to leave & told him I was getting a divorce & it was my attitude. No one in this town is to be trusted. You have to send them directly to my house. This doctor has nothing to say about my life & he thinks he is getting sued. I haven't seen this doctor & I have lost all respect for him. he wants me to loose the part on Dallas. He said it will never happen & tells the whole city & brags to his friends how he has stopped me. Who does he think he is! I will tell you why he wants me to loose the part. I told Leo a long time ago I hated the part. I took my friend to the emergency room & Leo & the doctor the psychiatrist tricked me into a emergency room pretending that my friend needed me blocked the door & was going to put me in the psychiatric ward because I told Leo I had a part on Dallas. I begged to let me go. Everybody knows I had the part!"

genuine fans with a desire to reach out and get as close as they could to their perceived hero, the majority of the mail was downright dizzy. We've all heard horror stories about stars being hounded by obsessed fans.

To. Mr Johnnie Carson
+ Ed Mchanton

This is my Bank Teller

Please let her ~~Know~~ Know or inform her about ~~B~~ Me :

This sign is for

Female's = Mother's Queens & Ladies of the Lord

Male's = King's or Fathers and Man of The Lord

I Now Pronoun you as

The Man of The Lord

They or over my Kings

My Late Grandmother Use to Whatch your Show every Night. Her Name Was [redacted] of Louisville

8-16-10

To 5 4 87 [scribbled out] word

And, while we don't want to dwell on the sorry, sad or sick, those letters were a part of the daily mail delivery. Without wanting to exploit some of the people who wrote on a regular basis, we felt it was important to include some "off-the-wall" letters in this book.

"To Mr. [Johnnie] Carson & Ed [McHanton],

This is my Bank Teller, please let her know or inform her about me. This sign is for Females = Mothers, Queens & Ladies of the Lord. Males = Kings or/and Fathers Man of the Lord.

I now [pronoun] you as The Man of the Lord.

They or over my Kings.

My late Grandmother use to Watch your show every night. Her name was [ ] of Louisville 8-16-10 to 5487. Please say [Grandmothers name] late [ ] of Louisville GA. on T.V. when you get time.

Thank you and have a good day, Bye ya'll."

Old Friends

Over the years, many of the same fans would write regularly to Johnny as if he were a relative or a close friend. We even began recognizing the names and the handwriting on the envelopes. In some strange way, these "regulars" became our old friends; each letter giving us an update about the events in their lives. Sadly, many of these regulars were profoundly lonely or suffered from mental problems. Every day, while

Dear Mr Carson

I am the second coming of Christ, The Messiah, the Son of the living God, and I can prove it!

I would be happy to come on your show either preach or be iddacuted. That decission would be entirely your peragative.

Sincerely

AKA Jesus Christ

mail

message

home

sorting through the mail, one of us would say, *"Oh, we got another one from so-and-so"* or *"So-and-so wrote three times this week!"*

Many of the letters we received were from the same women who routinely "fell in love" with Johnny. One woman wrote a steady stream of letters that always started out by saying that her bags were packed and she was waiting for Johnny to pick her up in his car. This same woman sent Johnny packaged undershirts, briefs, ties and dress shirts for many years.

We had our share of regulars who wrote to Johnny as if he were their parent or spouse. These were the letters that prompted us to contact the security department so that they could keep tabs on these individuals.

"I am the second coming of Christ, The Messiah, the Son of the living God, and I can prove it!

I would be happy to come on your show either [to] preach or be [riddaculed], that decision would be entirely your [perogative].

Sincerely,

[ ]

[ ] AKA Jesus Christ"

Money

Little money was sent to the show, as most people were requesting financial aid. We did however, receive a buck or two over the years. We always made it a practice to send the money back since Johnny always

Psychiatric
Institute

Dear Johnny,

Nobody likes me,
Everybody hates me,
I think I'll eat worms.
Nice big fat one
Juicy little skinny ones,
I like the way they wiggle and worm.

I'm very excited.

sent out his autograph *gratis.* We had a fellow write once a month who sent in $10 and started each letter, "Dear Dad, Here's the rent money this month. Love, Bob." There was never a return address so we just deposited the money in our private fund; those lunch prices in the NBC commissary went up every year! There was another viewer who belonged to a large organized religion who sent in a quarter, a few nickels, and a couple of pennies once or twice a week with the organization's pamphlet and a package of beef jerky. Not exactly hitting the jackpot.

"Nobody likes me,
Everybody hates me,
I think I'll eat worms. Nice big fat ones.
Juicy little skinny ones,
I like the way they wiggle and worm.
[ ]
I'm very excited."

Secret Service

Opening and answering the mail for a celebrity is fascinating and absorbing most of the time. Nonetheless, we must be perfectly honest and admit that at times, it can be scary and oppressive. We have both opened more than our share of ominous letters and have had experiences where we were actually

Dear Dad

How in the hell have you been doing?

Please don't tell anyone that I'm writting you this letter or the Parole Board will think that my schizophria is regressing and that I am having a relaps.

I know that I am not your adopted son, and that you did not adopt me when I was very young. The psyciatrist, in the prison that I was in, have convinced me that you and I have never even met.

But ya see Dad, Fathers Day is comming up in a few months, and I dont have anybody to send a fathers day card too. So even though I am not haveing a relaps in to the land of mental illness for some reason I really did feel like writting you a letter.

The kind that I use to WRITE TO you when I was in prison and thought I was funny. Well, I never though that I was funny but I use to think that the letters I wrote were, espicaly the letters about the frist family.

In case your wondering if I am trying to get something out of you, I promiss not to ask you for anything until after fathers day. And going by your past record I'll expect not to get any thing frightened by what the postman delivered. Once we received a box that contained an object that looked just like a homemade bomb, and yes, it *was* ticking. We called NBC security who sent for the local bomb squad. Fortunately, it turned out to be nothing more than an attention-getting device (which it did) by a man hoping to get booked on the show (which he didn't).

"Dear Dad,

How in the hell have you been doing?

Please don't tell anyone that I'm writing you this letter or the Parole Board will think that my [schizophria] is regressing and that I am having a [relaps].

I know that I am not your adopted son, and that you did not adopt me when I was very young. The [psyciatrist], in the prison that I was in, [have] convinced me that you and I have never even met.

But ya see Dad, Father's Day is [comming] up in a few months, and I don't have anybody to send a fathers day card too. So even though I am not [haveing] a [relaps] in to the land of mental illness for some reason I really did feel like writing you a letter.

The kind that I use to write to you when I was in prison and thought I was funny. Well, I never thought that I was funny but I use to think that the letters I wrote were [espicaly] the letters about the first family.

In case your wondering if I am trying to get something out of you, I promise not to ask you for anything until after fathers day. And going by your past record, I'll expect not to get any thing."

Dear Johnny

"My resume"

If I was a mop bucket would you love me? But a mop bucket ain't what I'd like to be. But I'd like to get on at NBC doing some thing behind the scenes nonsense. Why? To live in Cal and make enough bucks to afford food and shelter at least. This place sucks.

If I don't hear from you. I'll be in school September. I'd like a degree too.

Have pencil - will write.

The Sorcerers

apprentice

Love You

Jall!

Yours truly

Love [redacted]

P.S. Be home two weeks from today

april 26th '91

A few years ago, it seemed that letter-bombs were all the rage, and consequently, we were given instructions

"1. My resume.

If I was a mop bucket would you hire me? But a mop bucket ain't what I'd like to be. But I'd like to get on at NBC doing something behind the scenes nonsense. Why? To live in Cal and make enough bucks to afford food and shelter at least. This place sucks.

If I don't hear from you.

I'll be in school September.

I'd like a degree too.

Have pencil - will write.

The Sorcerers Apprentice

Yours truly

Love you Jay!

P.S. Be home two weeks from today April 26th 91."

on how to identify potentially explosive deliveries. All celebrities receive letters from the fringe of society and they should never be taken lightly. Many of the same people wrote to Johnny regularly and some were considered dangerous. We usually passed these letters on to law enforcement officials and investigators who tracked stalkers and obsessed fans. We've spoken to police departments in many cities across the United States to inform them that a local citizen had been writing questionable letters.

PROBLEM DENTURES?
Longs
$2.39
Take a bite out of life.
ezo 12 UPPER HEAVY DENTURE CUSHIONS
Johnny - Try one, two or three of these in your upper plate. Easy to install if warmed first.

Whenever we received such a letter from a prospective stalker, it was our task to inspect the postmark to determine if he/she was getting any closer to the Los Angeles area. We did have a few incidents over the years at the NBC studios, but fortunately, no one was ever hurt.

"Johnny - Try one, two or three of these in your upper plate. Easy to install if warmed first."

Some viewers thought Johnny had a lisp and would often suggest various treatments.

1 II Dec [redacted]

Johnny Carson has

proof my wife at

(213) [redacted]

will destroy Burbank

with an earthquake

on or before X-mas

Day —

8

"Johnny Carson has proof my wife at (213) [   ] will destroy Burbank with an earthquake on or before X-mas Day.

[signed, 8-Ball]"

MAY 13

DEAR JOHNNY,

I KILLED KING ARTHUR BY EXCALIBUR. I TRIED TO MARRY [redacted] AGAIN. YOU WERE NOT IN THE TUBES.

SINCERELY,

"I killed King Arthur by Excalibur. I tried to marry [ ] again. You were not in the tubes."

DEAR JOHN,

I AM STUCK IN A MENTAL HOSPITAL AGAIN. ACTUALLY I'M AT THE

THE BOREDOM IS OVERWHEMING. THEY DON'T LET US STAY UP LATE ENOUGH TO WATCH "THE TONIGHT SHOW". DON'T YOU THINK THAT'S CRUEL AND UNUSUAL PUNISHMENT. BESIDES, I HAVEN'T EVEN DONE ANYTHING WRONG. BUT THE WORST

"I am stuck in a mental hospital again. Actually I'm at [ ]
The boredom is overwhelming. They DON'T let us stay up late enough to watch "The Tonight Show". Don't you think that's cruel and unusual punishment. Besides, I haven't even done anything wrong. But the worst is they are rationing my cigarette smoking. Don't you just want to sue their butts off?

Your Pal."

South Central Bell
A BELLSOUTH Company

SUMMARY OF CHARGES BILLED

CURRENT CHARGES
SOUTH CENTRAL BELL 44.47
SOUTH COMMUNICATIONS 2.43
AT&T ... CHARGES 46.90
... AFTER JUL 08 *** TOTAL AMOUNT DUE 46.90

South Central Bell
P.O. Box 39
Nashville, Tennessee 37202

U.S. POSTAGE 0.17
745581

Hello my precious little Hubby
I hope when these few lines reach
you they will find you in good
health and myself likewise. Sweet
heart I'm already packed and
waiting on you to send Pinaks
Slov after me. I'm ready to come
to you whenever you send for me
anytime after Aug. I'm sending
you my rent receipt so you will
know how much rent I pay. I
know you love me and I do love
you sweet heart. You and I might
build and live here in [redacted].
I'm sorry about the tornado
you all had. I believe you will make
me a good husband. A thousand kisses
to you. I'm closing my letter but
not my heart.

"Hello my precious little Hubby, I hope when these few lines reach you they will find you in good health and myself likewise, Sweetheart I'm already packed and waiting on you to send Dinah Shore[?] after me, I'm ready to come to you whenever you send for me anytime after Aug, I'm sending you my rent receipt so you well know how much rent I pay. I know you love me and I do love you sweetheart. You and I might build and live here in [ ]. I'm sorry about the tornado you all had. I believe you will make me a good husband. A thousand kisses to you. I'm enclosing my letter but not my heart."

This fan, who thought Johnny was her husband, wrote at least once a month and always included her telephone bill.

Thursday

Hi Johnny,

I heard you mention you had a desire to be a "sniper" as a kid on your show. You asked for no letters on the subject so thats why I wrote you one.

I wanted to be a rapist but I grew up to become a bank-robber and now I'm contemplating what to do next as I "get out" next year.

I did 7 years for sticking guns in peoples faces but sex is the crime of the 80s child abuse, rape, child molestation etc. ect. etc.

So I don't know; I feel out of place being a bank-robber from 1979. I guess I shouda waited another year.

Being around all these skinners for the past 7+ years is hell. I think maybe I made a mistake.

Mothers guard your daughters. and young mothers beware.

Only because I don't know what I want to be when I grow up.

A "fan"

"I heard you mention you had a desire to be a "sniper" as a kid on your show. You asked for no letters on the subject so that's why I wrote you one.

I wanted to be a rapist but I grew up to become a bank-robber and now I'm contemplating what to do next as I "get out" next year.

I did 7 years for sticking guns in peoples faces but sex is the crime of the 80s child abuse, rape, child molestation etc, [ect], etc.

So I don't know; I feel out of place being a bank-robber from 1979. I guess I [shouda] waited another year.

Being around all these skinners for the past 7+ years is hell. I think maybe I made a mistake.

Mothers guard your daughters and young mothers beware.

Only because I don't know what I want to be when I grow up.

A "fan" "

be my father not
my Mother!

You may be nuts! but
your still my Daddy

Sometimes,
even my teddy bear
didn't understand...
but you always did.
Thanks, Dad.

HAPPY FATHER'S DAY
WITH LOVE

and I still love
you!

"Be my father not my mother!

You may be nuts! But your still my Daddy and I still love you!"

CONFIDENTIAL - JOHNNY CARSON
EYES ONLY.

Dear John the Divine,

Please take this message seriously. I am Jesus, re-incarnate. And you are John the Divine, and David Letterman, is the root of David, I have arrived. Please read this on your show and show the picture, please. Remember, God has a sense of humor and we are all to be like and unto God the Father and Heavenly Mother.

P.S. Make a joke of this, I would. ~ Jesus ~
- Stranger than Truth

Chapter Eight Religious Fanatics

Opening letters from those who truly believed that they were either God, Jesus, or Satan himself was typical. While it is obvious that those letters were from deranged individuals, we were constantly astounded at the number of writers who wanted to convert Johnny. Each day, we opened at least ten letters from people quoting the scriptures. It seems there's an appropriate psalm for every joke Johnny told as well as every event that happened in his life.

"Dear John the Divine,

Please take this message seriously. I am Jesus, re-incarnate And you are John the Divine, and David Letterman, is the root of David, I have arrived. Please read this on your show and show the picture, please. Remember, God has a sense of humor and we are all to be like and unto God the Father and Heavenly Mother.

P.S. Make a joke of this, I would. – Stranger than Truth."

Many of the "preachy" writers sent letters at least three or four times a week. We had one fan who sent us a quarter with every letter and also included pamphlets promoting his belief. Over the years we received hundreds of Bibles, bottles of holy water, bags of "Holy Dirt," and all sorts of religious propaganda. We suppose it was some comfort to know that people were out there praying for the show.

Post Script:

Dear Johnny Carson,

How would a Calvinist say a final, final last Goodbye?

Answer: the same way they would say hello when you are born.

I: Here is your armor, the 23d Psalm.
It will be your protection and safeguard.
A table has been prepared for you in the presence of your enemies
and
You will walk through the valley of the shadow of death
however
You will fear no evil because goodness and mercy will follow you
and
You will dwell in the house of the Lord forever.

II Remember the legend of Robert Bruce and the spider.

III Watch for the Lady in the Lake.

"How would a Calvinist say a final, final last goodbye?

Answer: The same way they would say hello when you are born.

I. Here is your armor, the 23rd Psalm. It will be your protection and safeguard. A table has been prepared for you in the presence of your enemies and you will walk through the valley of the shadow of death however, you will fear no evil because goodness and mercy will follow you and you will dwell in the house of the Lord forever.

II. Remember the legend of Robert Bruce and the spider.

III. Watch for the Lady in the Lake. How would a methodist say a final, final last goodbye? They would say, Thank you, Johnny Carson. "For now we see through a glass darkly; but then face to face: Now I know in part; but then shall I know even as also I am known. And now abideth faith, hope, charity, these three; but the greatest of these is charity."

Post Script:

The final questions from a Calvinist:

I. Virginia, did you see the Lady in the Lake?

Answer: Yes, Sir, I believe I saw the meaning of it.

II. Did she give you the Excalibur?

Answer: Yes, Sir, it is my belief that she did.

Final Questions form a Methodist:

They would not ask any questions they do not go inside of someone's mind, it is Contrary to their teachings."

International Flavor

Despite the fact that the "Tonight Show" was only seen in the United States and Canada, we received letters from all over the world in different languages.

Dear Johnny,
It's difficult to know just how to word this letter.
I am a forty year old widow – married 15 years to a wonderful man 22 years my senior. He was killed 5 years ago in a horse-back riding accident. I have one 17 yr old son.
Although I have not been able to watch your show regularly, many times I have, through the years, "laughed until I cried" at your great humor.
This past week, as I have watched your last few shows – I have felt a sadness for myself and your fans. But then I think – what about you?
I know your life has been difficult – I know fame and fortune have absolutely nothing to do with happiness.
There is, however, a way to find happiness, even in this

"It's difficult to know just how to word this letter. I am a forty year old widow - married 15 years to a wonderful man 22 years my senior. He was killed 5 years ago in a horse-back riding accident. I have one 17 yr old son.

Although I have not been able to watch your show regularly, many times I have, through the years, "laughed until I cried" at your great humor.

This past week, as I have watched your last few shows, I have felt a sadness for myself and your fans. But then I think, what about you?

I know your life has been difficult, I know fame and fortune have absolutely nothing to do with happiness.

There is, however, a way to find happiness, even in this very wicked system of things we find ourselves in.

The key to happiness, Johnny, is very simply, Do things God's way.

As one of Jehovah's Witnesses, I have found conclusively that this is the only formula that works in every aspect of life.

Perhaps you have known of the Witnesses before my letter; if not I hope you will take the time to read the enclosed tract. It contains information that is most comforting to those of us who have lost loved ones in death.

I've enclosed a picture of myself taken on vacation in San Diego; so that you know I'm a plain old East Texas country girl with no ulterior motive other than to help a very humble and meek person find "the truth that sets one free".

I will be in SFO June 10-19. I would be happy to meet with you and help get you on the road to real happiness & security through a closer relationship with our creator, Jehovah God.

Christian love & affection."

Greetings Johnny

It is the Mother with the Sons. Isa 54:5-17

I'm taking a walk and asking JehoVah God what is it that you want Johnny to know, before finishing this letter. This is what JehoVah wants you to know, I am having a strong fight spiritually. Daniel 10:12 And he went on to say to me: Do not be afraid, O Daniel, for ~~your~~ from the first day that you gave your heart to understanding and humbling yourself before your God your words have been heard, and I myself have come because of your words,

Daniel prayed at his laddice

But the prince of the royal realm of Persia was standing in opposition to me for twenty one days, and, look! Michael, one of the foremost princes, came to help me; and I for my part, remained there beside the king of Persia. JehoVah does love you Johnny, because I prayed to JehoVah. O please who will really be agreeable to your heart, and no matter how, difficult + bitter or distressed one can be, because not everyday is our day, that he would stay with you JehoVah, and JehoVah kept showing me Johnny with the angel on his head meaning, devine words are coming from JehoVah God Almighty.

This was not a common occurrence, but we did get one or two a week. We had letters from past viewers who were stationed overseas, unable to watch the show, who actually had friends or relatives send them tapes of the program to watch so that they wouldn't lose touch with Johnny's monologue.

"Greetings Johnny,

It is the Mother with the Sons. [Isa] 54: 5-17. [Im] taking a walk and asking Jehovah God what is it that you want Johnny to know, before finishing this letter. This is what Jehovah wants you to know. I am having a strong fight spiritually.

Daniel 10:12 And he went on to say to me: Do not be afraid, O Daniel, for from the first day that you gave your heart to understanding and humbling yourself before your God your words have been heard, and I myself have come because of your words, Daniel prayed at his [laddice]. I myself have come because of your words, But the prince of the royal realm of Persia was standing in opposition to me for twenty one days, and, look! Michael, one of the foremost princes, came to help me; and I for my part, remained there beside the king of Persia. Jehovah does love you Johnny, because I prayed to Jehovah.

O please who will really be agreeable to your heart and no matter how, difficult & bitter or distressed one can be, because not everyday is our day, that he would stay with you Jehovah and Jehovah kept showing me Johnny with the Angel on his head meaning, [devine] words are coming from Jehovah God [allmighty]."

This person wrote every week and always included a quarter (and sometimes some added loose change) glued to the letter and a package of beef jerky.

Mr. Johnny Carson
c/o Tonight Show
NBC
3000 W. Alameda Ave.
Burbank, California 91523

Dear Mr. Carson (Johnny):

Let me introduce myself simply as a Catholic Christian woman, a person who wishes you to know that I do pray for you. I am following up on a thought or plan of a friend of mine, a man who told a group of us he was going to write to you to inform you that he was praying for you. To my knowledge he did not do this because he met with an accident (he fell off a roof) and died. If he had not mentioned this, I would not be writing to you today.

Most of us have been asked at sometime by other people to pray for them. You have not asked but I do wish you to know that I do pray for you.

I ask you to consider 2 things:

1. Is Jesus Christ a real person in your life?

2. If you asked the Lord for something, for what would you ask?

Do take the time to think about these 2 considerations.

Enclosed is a picture of the risen Jesus.

If you wish, please reply.

GOD BLESS YOU,

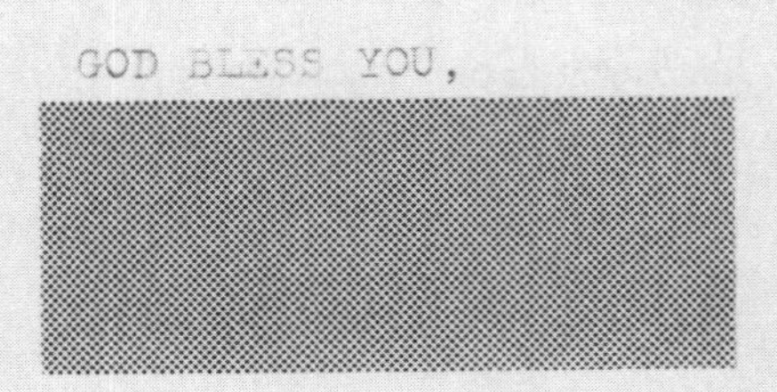

"Let me introduce myself simply as a Catholic Christian woman, a person who wishes you to know that I do pray for you. I am following up on a thought or plan of a friend of mine, a man who told a group of us he was going to write to you to inform you that he was praying for you. To my knowledge he did not do this because he met with an accident (he fell off a roof) and died. If he had not mentioned this, I would not be writing to you today.

Most of us have been asked at sometime by other people to pray for them. You have not asked but I do wish you to know that I do pray for you.

I ask you to consider 2 things:

1. Is Jesus Christ a real person in your life?

2. If you asked the Lord for something, for what would you ask?

Do take the time to think about these 2 considerations.

Enclosed is a picture of the risen Jesus.

If you wish, please reply.

GOD BLESS YOU"

October 7, 1991

Dear Johnny,

I am a 51 Year old (White) lady, in a Partnership Restaurant, With my husband of 32 Years. In all My Years of observing talented People, I've Never seen one that I Would put My personal stamp of approval on, to the extent that I Would Write to Johnny Carson for help.

I have recently seen such a person. He is a 16 Year old (White) Youth, Who is so good, you Would Not believe it! This person needs to be on Your show. He is only a short-time from being known, Whether he gets on Your show or Not. My husband & I have seen him perform twice. His Mother says he started at age 3. She has pictures of him holding a pencil as a Microphone. He seems to have Plenty of self-Confidence & is such an affecionate Person, that I saw him hug elderly (80 +) People. Small Children love him, so his Mother has said.

If there is Any Way We Could help this talented Person, We Certaintly Would appricate anything or Any direction You Could lead us, that We might tell his Parents–

Thank You for Your time to read this. Sorry about Using linoleum but I Wanted to get Your attention.

Chapter Nine **Alternative Writing Surfaces**

Viewers took pen in hand to scribe their sentiments on paper towels, paper napkins, toilet and facial tissue, and place mats from fast-food restaurants. At times we read notes jotted down on the backs of bank deposit slips, telephone bills, or the inside cover of paperback books. Computer paper and the corner of a previously owned greeting card or letter seemed to be the stationery of choice for a multitude of fans. No surface was *verboten,* not even the back of a piece of kitchen

"I am a 51 year-old (white) lady in a Partnership Restaurant, With my husband of 32 years. In all my year of observing talented People, I've never seen one that I would put my personal stamp of approval on, to the extent that I would write to Johnny Carson for help.

I have recently seen such a person. He is a 16 year-old youth who is so good, you would not believe it! This person needs to be on your show. He is only a short-time from being known, Whether he gets on your show or not. My husband and I have seen him perform twice. His Mother says he started at age 3. She has pictures of him holding a pencil as a microphone. He seems to have plenty of self-confidence and is such an [affecionate] persson, that I saw him hug elderly (80+) people. Small children love him, so his mother has said.

If there is Any Way We Could help this talented Person, We Certainly Would appreciate anything or any direction you could lead us that We might tell his Parents.

Thank You for your time to read this. Sorry about using linoleum but I Wanted to get Your Attention."

This was one of the most unique writing surfaces that we had ever received. As you can tell from the front and back view of this letter, it *really* is linoleum.

A Holy man who [illegible] one of the 3 wise men [illegible]
John Lennon [illegible]
[illegible] Closet [illegible] with Albert Einstein
Frank Sinatra spends a lot of time [illegible] movies
Clayton Moore (Lone Ranger)
Jay Silverheels
Lassie, Benji
My Three [illegible]
[illegible] and Donna
President Gandhi
Mahatma Gandhi
Martin Luther King and family (He was [illegible] Luther)
Coretta King
Eleanor Roosevelt
("Dont let the last name [illegible]")
Teddy Roosevelt is Eleanor's uncle
Carol King
[illegible]

David Rockefeller gave the Rockefeller center to me while Jesus taken care of spiritual business [illegible] while I begin the streets.
Giving money [illegible] H. L. Hunt's son [illegible]
J. Paul Getty [illegible] my friend with God

Martha Raye
June Allyson
(Spelling is gone for the day)
Jack Douglas
Jack Paar
Debbie Reynolds
Laurence Olivier
Jose Feliciano
Foster Brooks
Esther Williams
Hedy Lamarr
Alan Ladd
Lynn Redgrave
Roy Orbison
Julia Child
Omar Sharif
Tom Selleck
[illegible]

(P.P.S. Here's SNAKE NATION - I was a finalist with my story but was not printed in the book - the OUTLINE FOR MY BOOK DEDICATED TO YOU)

Mr. Carson

(Please forward this to him.)

P.S. Here's a box of MEMORY Chocolates because we'll always remember YOU.
P.P.S. [illegible]

We look forward to one day meeting you. We would fly out for the show if we had the money.

As a child I watched you with my mom. Now my children continue to watch you with me.

This framed picture expresses our gratitude to you! This is not exactly your 30th anniversary for the Show HAPPY (almost) anniversary of the year & [illegible]

My children will miss you too.

This "ESSAY ON MAN" has to quote

"Hope Springs Eternal". You have always [illegible] hope & [illegible] it with HUMOR to [illegible] a garden of HAPPINESS!

You've been my "friend" & I hope you receive this! Here's a neat card, too: TAKE TIME. & THANKS

I used to live in Southern CA & have been in GA 9 years now. [illegible] I received $20,000 in Scholarships (the ROTAKY was one of them) [illegible] your [illegible]

"Big Blue Wrecking Crew"

Dear Tommy The woods are dark & lovely, & deep, but I have promises to keep, & miles & miles to go before I sleep.

And now I suppose you would like to know the layout of the town. I haven't been there since 19[illegible] [illegible] I saw only [illegible] mock-up of how it was when I left, I haven't been back since. So I suppose like all small towns the L-shaped layout would be the most appropriate. On [illegible] St., I guess it runs across we'll start from Grandma [illegible]'s house, there use to be a gas station across the street, a bridal shop owned by Butch Garlick's mother now directly across the street again was a hangout for kids, called B's. Further down, much further was Wolfe's bowling alley, (Dennis died in the service) was a friend of mine, then came Aunt Helen's house on Main Street. There was a place called [illegible] linoleum. Letters written on dirty paper stained with substances of unknown origins whispered to us, "Wear rubber gloves!"

Novels

Considering the volume of mail received, we always appreciated opening the letter that offered the sentiment, request, or criticism in the first sentence. In fact, we were always relieved to read a letter from a fan that stated their case in one *page*. However, this was rarely the case. The average letter ran two and a half pages, although letters that were 10 pages or more were not uncommon. From time to time, we actually had to plow through letters containing 50 pages or more. We just couldn't understand it. In today's busy world, it's difficult to find time to vacuum the house, let alone write a letter over 200 pages! Never let it be said that the art of letter writing is dead. Just ask a celebrity!

- **Top left –**
  an industrial paper towel
- **Bottom left –**
  a long roll of computer paper
- **Right –**
  a standard paper towel.

- **Top left –**
  This person wrote to Johnny constantly. Each letter was always written on an extremely long papertowel roll measuring at least 30 feet!

- **Bottom left –**
  This person wrote twice a week. Each letter was about 30 pages long, written in beautiful penmanship yet none of the sentences made any sense whatsoever.

- **Top right –**
  Can you imagine receiving all these letters in just *one* month?! Not impressed? Well… these were all written by the same person! We would actually receive ten or more letters a day. The total count was 360 when the show ended, totalling well over 2,000 pages.

- **Right bottom –**
  This vertical novel was made up of 3 letters per line and was written on a roll of paper only 3/4" wide, as long as a roll of toilet paper.

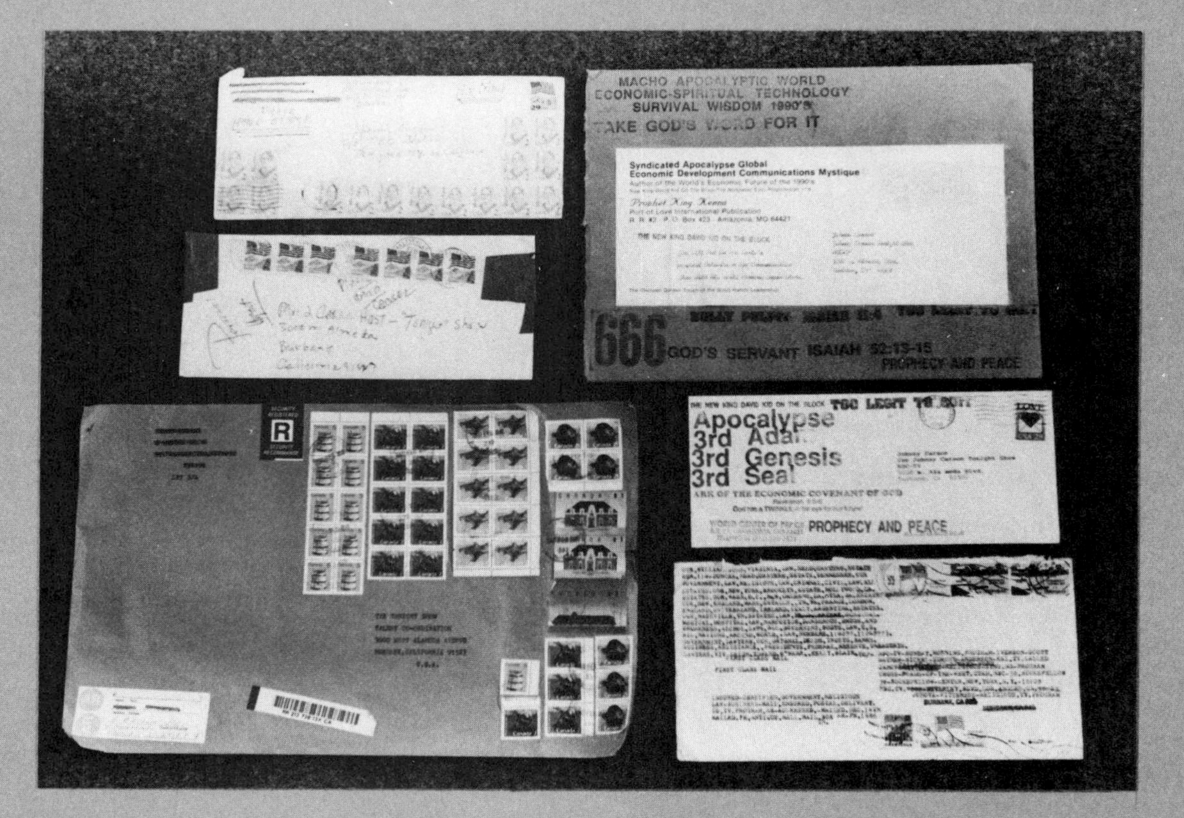

MACHO APOCALYPTIC WORLD
ECONOMIC-SPIRITUAL TECHNOLOGY
SURVIVAL WISDOM 1990'S
TAKE GOD'S WORD FOR IT
Syndicated Apocalypse Global
Economic Development Communications Mystique
Author of the World's Economic Future of the 1990's
666
GOD'S SERVANT ISAIAH 52:13-15
PROPHECY AND PEACE
THE NEW KING DAVID KID ON THE BLOCK
Apocalypse
3rd Genesis
3rd Seal
ARK OF THE ECONOMIC COVENANT OF GOD
PROPHECY AND PEACE

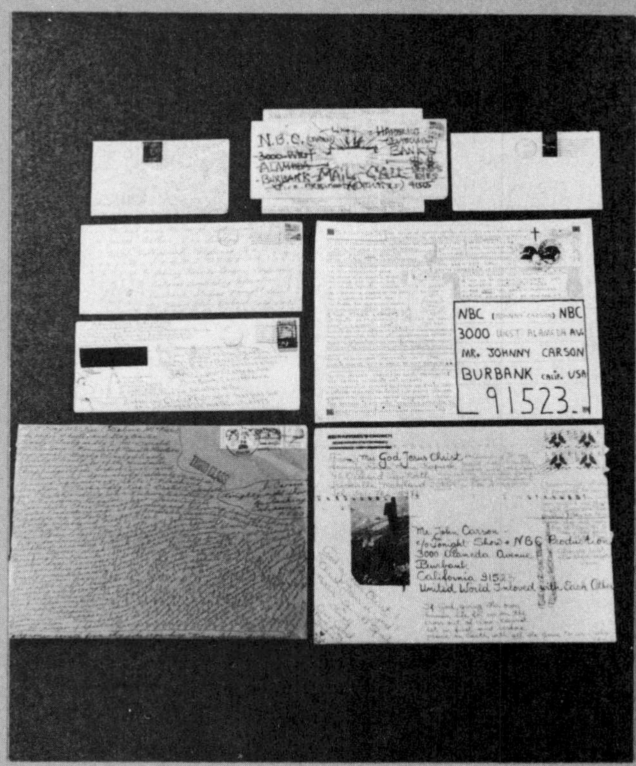

N.B.C.
MAIL CALL
NBC
NBC
3000
MR. JOHNNY CARSON
BURBANK
USA
91523.
Mr. John Carson
3000 Alameda Avenue
Burbank

Chapter Ten **Envelopes**

Many people would go to extremes to grab our attention by ornamenting the envelope of the letter or

- **TOP PHOTO –**
  - ***Envelopes on the left:*** **Many fans added extra postage to their letters to be assured that their letters wouldn't be returned for insufficient postage. These envelopes, all containing only one letter, had enough postage to go to Pluto. (The upper-left envelope was addressed by someone who couldn't make up his mind. On the last line which usually contains the city, state and zip, this fan wrote "New York or California." The postman flipped a coin and we won.)**
  - ***Upper right:*** **Just your average letter from Hades.**
  - ***Middle right:*** **Across the top of this envelope, written in very small print was "The New King David Kid-on-the-Block!"**
  - ***Lower right:*** **The second longest return address we had ever seen.**

- **BOTTOM PHOTO**
  - ***Upper left:*** **"Whew!" Finally, a normal envelope… and then we turned it over. There were at least 80 lines of completely illegible teeny handwriting filling the back of this small envelope. And once again, no letter inside.**
  - ***Second letter on the left:*** **The front of this envelope was loaded with Roman numerals. Maybe these are winning lotto numbers.**
  - ***Lower left:*** **"The Excedrin Envelope." No wonder there's so much stress among postal workers. Pity the postman trying to find the recipient's address in all this. And yes, that actually is some sort of return address!**
  - ***Top Middle:*** **This person couldn't make up his mind whether to send a letter or a postcard. So he glued a postcard on top of the envelope bearing a wildly multi-colored address.**
  - ***Top Right:*** **Ah, the minimalist. This envelope only said "Johnny Carson, New York." (The show was actually taped in California, but the simple style was a nice change just the same.)**
  - ***Bottom Right:*** **We never knew God was married, but his wife has been sending Johnny letters for years. Notice that the return address says "Mrs. God Jesus Christ."**

package they sent. On a daily basis we would open envelopes covered with drawings, unusual writing, stamps (both rubber and postage), photographs, glitter and bows, or cryptic messages. There were always those who chose not to write a letter. They just wrote directly on the envelope, jotting down their thoughts on the outside with absolutely nothing on the inside. We would actually be in receipt of letters lacking a complete address. They would read, "Johnny Carson, Burbank" or maybe just "Johnny Carson, U.S.A., Burbank" without the designation of a state but we still got 'em!

It was amazing that the rule and not the exception was to place excessive postage on the envelopes, possibly to insure delivery. Some of the letters we received over the years had enough postage to go to the moon and back! Since many of the extra stamps weren't cancelled at the post office, we rarely had to purchase our own.

The Door

Traditionally, the most outrageous letter we received that week had the dubious honor of being posted on our door. Some weeks there were so many "winners" the door seemed to be camouflaged in paper of various colors. Each morning, with coffee mug in hand, members of our staff would typically stop by and "read" our door, much like you'd read the morning paper. Our co-workers always asked if they could make copies of the letters for their family and friends who might find the "Tonight Show" mailbag hard to believe!

Thank You,
JOHNNY CARSON
HEEERRE'SS
JOHNNY!
DIBUJO y BORDADO por
"El Guapo"
JOHNNY

Chapter Eleven Objets d'Art

Fans expended an enormous amount of energy and time to express their affection toward Johnny through art. On a regular basis, we received a multitude of expensively framed portraits of Johnny, rendered in just about every possible medium: crochet, pen and ink, chalk, watercolor, pencil, crayon, etc.

Likenesses of Johnny arrived daily in the form of portraits. Every level of artist sent in a rendition of what the official Johnny Carson portrait should be. We must admit that many were phenomenal, catching the features and the essence of the man who sat behind the desk for so many years. Others were pretty good, as we could identify them as being a sketch or painting of Johnny. And then there were our favorites, the surrealist and the abstract; those free expressions trying to convey raw unbridled emotion about the "Tonight Show" host. Those were the paintings that raised the question, "Who is this supposed to be?"

Aspiring illustrators didn't stop at drawing Johnny. They sculpted his image in clay and iron, twisted it in used coat hangers and sewed it from scraps of fabric. Johnny wasn't always the subject of their creation, however. Objects of art that defied description lined the walls and bookshelves of the mail room. From the wet, newly-painted, 50-foot canvas to the sculptures no larger than the head of a pin, the procession of eccentric creations continued. As we approached the last show, the aforementioned wet 50-footer seemed to duplicate itself; one arriving every week by the same artist! We only wished he'd waited until the paint

JOHNNY CARSON
Thanks for the 30
1962–1992
JOHNNY CARSON
GOLDEN FOOT-IN-MOUTH AWARD
Presented to
JOHNNY CARSON
for outstanding achievement
in saying the wrong thing
at the wrong time
Johnny's
RETIREMENT
clock
JOHNNY CARSON
HEEERRE'SS
JOHNNY!
DIBUJO Y BORDADO POR
"El Guapo"
EL PASO, TEXAS

dried! The artist spent an absolute fortune on postage. Strange gifts that sat in our office provided fodder for conversation, and again that age old question came up, *"Why?"*

Photographs

People sent in photographs of themselves in large numbers. It didn't matter how old they were, or how young, whether they were dressed or undressed, fit or flabby. Viewers sent them in daily by the hundreds. Many memorable photos come to mind but the ones that stand out include the pictorial essay of a man's gunshot wound to the head; an older man who was butt-naked standing in the woods holding a chain saw (it was a great looking chain saw!), and the 8x10 of a woman in the same state of undress as *"Mr. Outdoors"* in a bathtub holding a wine glass.

Fellow staff members were constantly amazed that people would have the guts to send, with absolutely no shame or embarrassment, a cheesecake photo of themselves. Students also included their class photo with their letters and others signed their portrait as if *they* were the celebrity signing a publicity shot for Johnny to frame and hang on *his* wall.

- **Top Left Photo – A "foot" stool atop a brick carved out with Johnny's name.**
- **Bottom Left Photo – An actual working clock which someone created out of plaster of Paris.**
- **Top Right Photo – We received many trophies and awards for Johnny, but a "Golden Foot-in-Mouth Award?"**
- **Bottom Right Photo – A carefully embroidered and framed plaque.**

MISTER BEDROOM
BOB HOPE
BURT REYNOLDS
DICK CAVETT
TINY TIM
NBC
FREDDIE
NIGHTIME

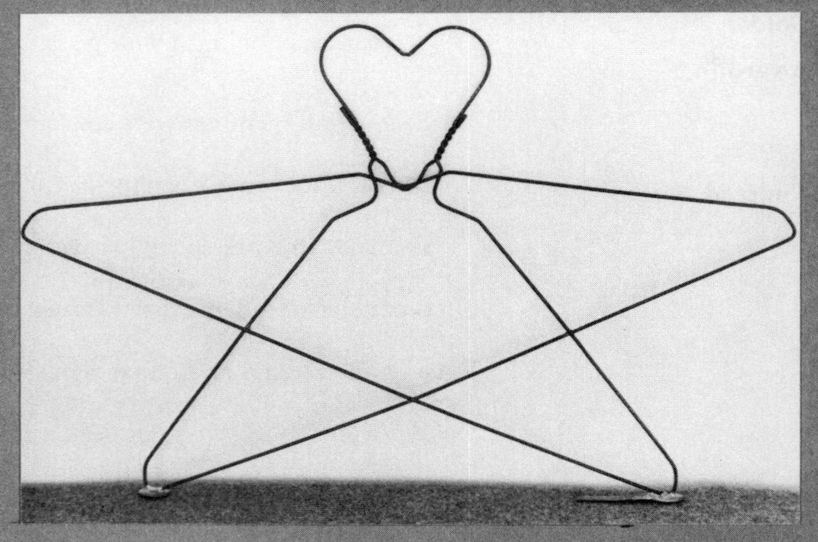

We were surprised that the majority of photographs we received were of children and pets watching Johnny on TV. We were particularly astonished at the number of photos of outhouses across the land with signs reading, "Here's Johnny!" It also seemed that Carson was a popular name for cities and towns because we received a shot from every community, minuscule and mighty.

Many fans sent snapshots of the interiors of their homes. We felt like voyeurs spying on different people's living habits. We daresay the main motivation in sharing a likeness or image was to be a guest on the program, but some sincerely wanted to give Johnny a part of themselves or to simply be part of *his* life.

- **Top Photo – A work of art in brass depicting people and places associated with the "Tonight Show" family, Johnny's staff, his hometown, and even the word "sex" tucked away in the upper left.**
- **Bottom Photo – The artist of this creation phoned us constantly to check if we had received his "metal sculpture." After making room for its arrival, we were rather surprised to discover that it was nothing more than two coat hangers that had been soldered together.**

Safe Sex

Starting in the mid 1980's, when the frightening reality of AIDS started a condom resurgence, there was a constant stream of novelty condoms arriving at our office daily in every possible form. We saw condom jewelry, condom trees, condom cartoon characters, colored condoms, colossal condoms, and even a Saddam Hussein condom for the lawless lover.

HOW
HOT
IS
IT?

T-shirts

Just about every metropolis and organization on the planet produced a T-shirt for their local event or cause and sent it to Johnny to display on the air. From the "Artichoke Festival" to the "Plumbers Convention," from the "Save the Minks" campaign to the "Stop the War" movement, T-shirts arrived by the truckloads for Johnny.

Hats

We received thousands of hats and caps over the years, some bearing working gadgets, trinkets, yo-yo's, and more. All had something to do with the show or something Johnny may have said during his monologue.

Johnny simply couldn't store the number of hats that barraged the office each day, so we gave the surplus hats and caps to Fred deCordova, our executive producer. (Fred was known for putting on the more bizarre ones and parading up and down the office to show them off.) We were sent an endless supply of novelty caps that boasted blinking lights and working parts, clocks, stuffed animal appendages, and who-knows-what.

The "Teeth"

As we have mentioned, it was impossible to keep every item or letter that was sent to Johnny. We simply didn't have the storage space to accommodate the mounds of mail and all the quirky contraptions. Over the years, we gave away a lot of "things" and threw

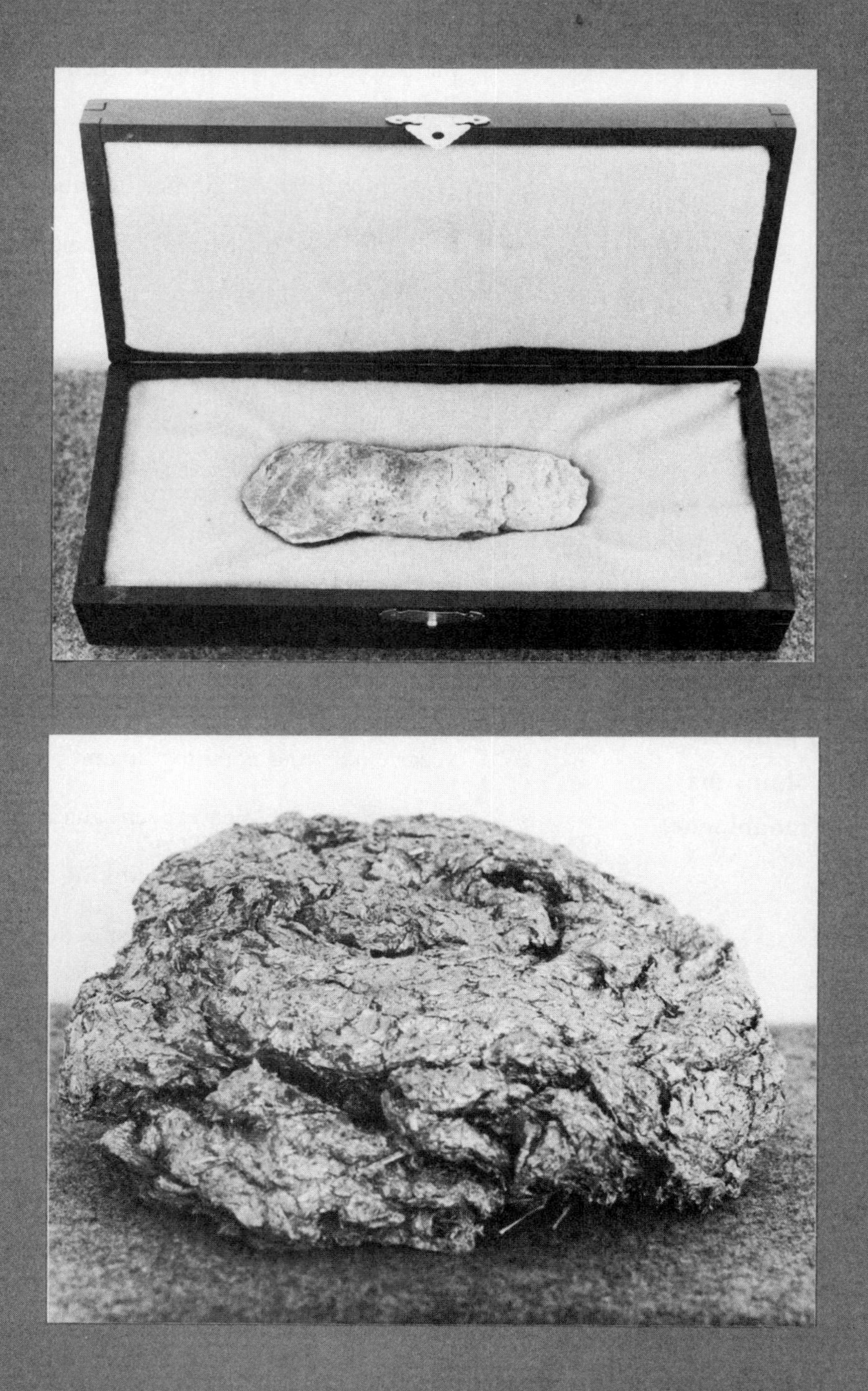

away just as many. Therefore, in the preparation of this book, as were were plowing through the drifts of letters and stacks of art, we would remember those prized gifts that Johnny received, but we didn't save. One item we regret not having saved was "the teeth." A dentist sent Johnny a 20"x36" fiber board decorated with 16 complete dentures (uppers *and* lowers) that were horribly contorted, all coated with thick white paint that dried with the drips intact. This was supposed to be a parody on the "Talk Show"... get it? We hung on to this chef d'oeuvre for a few years, being forced to answer at least a million times, *"... We don't know why!"* to the many visitors in our office who wanted to know the reason behind sending something so bizarre-looking. Finally, after one of our spring cleanings, it left for the NBC landfill museum.

- **Top Photo –**
  Ahhh, the perfect gift: a petrified doberman dropping placed carefully in a felt-lined box.

- **Bottom Photo –**
  This one has to take the cake: cow dung spray-painted gold. What does one do with cow dung spray-painted gold? Use it as a paper-weight? A doorstop? A brooch?

Fun With Feces

With seeming regularity, Johnny's mail bag often contained excrement, yes, excrement, molded and formed into possibly useful household or gift items such as paperweights, clocks or wall plaques.

We were dumfounded at the fascination with dung as a form of art. Cow and horse dung were the most popular media for clocks and sculptures, but no animal in the kingdom was exempt. Over the years we were the

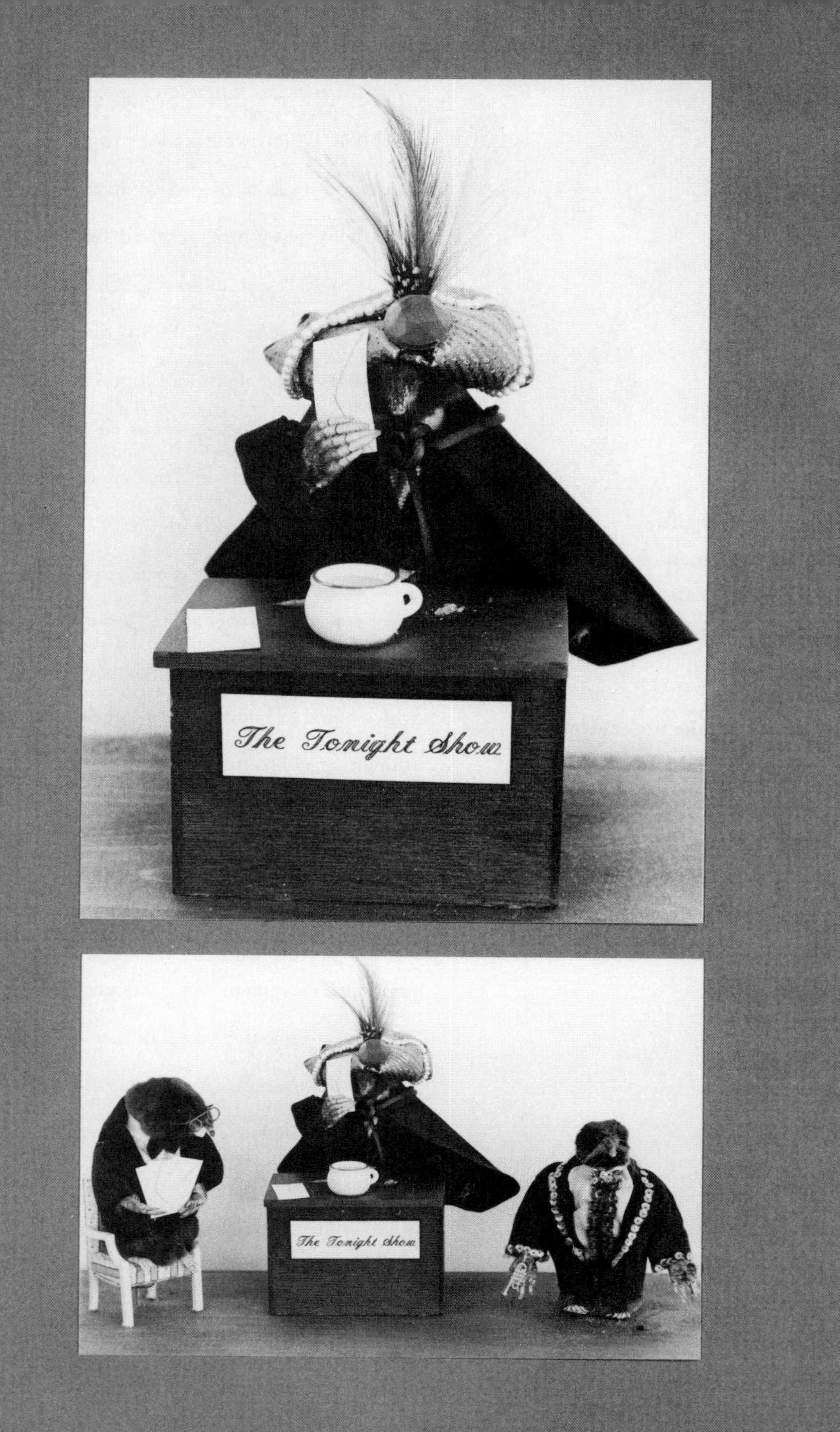

The Tonight Show
The Tonight Show

"fortunate" recipients of bird-dropping earrings, a doberman-dump that was carefully placed in a gray felt-lined box and from our fans in Florida, crocodile-caca in the shape of a heart that boasted the words, "We Love You, Johnny." So the next time you find a tiger-turd or pigeon-plop, just let it dry, shellac it and proudly send it along to your favorite talk-show host.

It's not your imagination. These are actual animals which have been stuffed and placed in various positions, recreating the set of the "Tonight Show." In the bottom photo, we have (from left to right) Ed holding envelopes which he is passing to Johnny dressed as Carnac. Doc is standing to the far right ready to play a tune on the trumpet he's holding in his right hand, ...ummm, claw.

HERE'S JOHNNY
HERE'S JOHNNY
THE CARSON CURTAIN
UP
DOWN
TO OPERATE STAGE

- **Top Photo –**
  Front view of an electric mock stage which was sent by a fan. When activated, the clay figure of Johnny comes out from behind the curtain and stops at the front of the stage.

- **Bottom Photo –**
  This back view shows the elaborate electrical system created for this gift. It always amazed us how much time (and money) viewers spent in order to impress Johnny.

March 27 1992

Dear Mr. Carson

I think you are a very good comdion person. When you retire I think you should be a T V talk show host.

Your friend

Chapter Twelve Kids Says the Most Honest Things

Children of all ages wrote to Johnny Carson and certainly contributed to the number of letters we read each day. Mostly they wanted an autograph, but many times they were requesting that Johnny help them with their class project or homework. We had many appeals for advice and biographies from youngsters aspiring to follow in Johnny's comic footsteps. Teachers would flood our office with letters that their students wrote to Johnny on a wide variety of subjects, and often these letters were read on the air. By far the greatest number of letters received by children were recipes (or their interpretation of recipes), that they enjoyed at the family table. The first ten were cute, however, after opening the 300th in a month, we weren't laughing at the kid whose recipe for bread was putting a sack of flour and a stick of butter in the oven.

"I think you are a very good [comidion] [persom]. When you retire I think you should be a T.V. talk-show host."

Senior Citizens

As every loyal viewer of the "Tonight Show" knows, Johnny was a real fan and admirer of this country's inspirational elderly. There were many astounding older folks on the program over the years, and practically every viewer who knew someone over 80

March 27, 1992

Dear Mr. Carson

Why are you retiring at
this time? Well let's get on
with it. Maybe you could be
a bus driver I dont no
anything else I tried

Your friend,

felt their friend or relative would make an ideal guest. We did find guests among the fan mail, but out of a hundred requests, probably only one or two would qualify for being quirky enough. Obviously, the "Tonight Show" was a comedy show and laughs were the goal.

"Why are you retiring at this time? Well let's get on with it. Maybe you could be a bus driver I [dont] [no] anything else I tried"

We received the most magnificent crochet work in the form of doilies and afghans (one afghan was in the pattern of the American flag and the size of a bedspread), knitted hats and scarves, and finely crafted wooden sculptures that were certainly the work of a perfectionist.

Then there was the mail from seniors that really touched our hearts; the mail from the lonely retirees who watched Johnny every night and felt he was their best friend.

Date March 27

Dear Mr. Carson,

We watched some of your show in class. It was interesting watching it in class. I never got to see it beacuse it was on too late. I think you should take naps and watch T.V. and read when you retire.

Your friend,

"We watched some of your show in class. It was interesting watching it in class. I never got to see it [beacuse] it was on too late I think you should take naps and watch T.V. and read when you retire"

sat March 24th

Dear Mr Carson:

My teacher taped your sho

I liked it couse it wuse

fanny I ust to stay up

and wotch you shoes

I stile do sometimes

wotch them I gust wunt

to give you some ideas

w write you do sents

you are retring you can stae

up late and wotch TV or you can

"My teacher taped [your'e] [shoe] I liked it [cause] it [wuse] funny I [ust] to [stae] up and [wotch] [you] [shoes] I still do [sone times] [wotch] them I [gust] [wunt] to give you some ideas We write you We do [sents] you are [retring] you can [stae] up late and [wotch] T.V. or you can rent a tape and [wotch] it I like [wotching] movies"

Dear Mr. Carson,

What are you going to do since you are retiring? I might have some suggestions. Maybe you can be a funny person on a show, but on a different show.

Your freind,

"What are you going to do since you are retiring? I might have some suggestions. Maybe you can be a funny person on a show, but on a different show."

March 27, 1992

Dear Mr. Carson,
Hi my name is
I heard you are going to retire.
I have some ideas for you to
do when you retire.
1. You might want to relax for
awhile.
2. Or you might want to spend
some time with your family.

"Hi my name is [ ]. I heard you are going to retire. I have some ideas for you to do when you retire.

1. *You might want to relax for a while.*
2. *Or you might want to spend some time with your family.*
3. *You might want to watch re-runs of your shows.*

Well I'll talk to you later."

March 27 1992

Dear Ms. Carson,
We saw you on the T.V.
Maybe you could get a
job fixing cars.

Your friend

"*We saw you on the T.V. Maybe you could get a job fixing cars.*"

March 27, 1992

Dear Mr. Corson

When you retire I have somethings that you can do.

Read, listen to music, watch TV, stay up late, make your own joke book.

Your friend,

"When you retire I have [somethings] that you can do. Read, listen to music, watch TV, stay up late, make your own Joke book."

Sing to the tune of "Oh Johnny"

Oh Johnny

Oh Johnny, Oh Johnny
Say it's not true.
Oh Johnny, Oh Johnny
How I'll miss you.
I spend my nights in ecstacy.
With my remote, a beer and
good old N.B.C.EEEE —
Oh Johnny, Oh Johnny
What will I do.
I can't go to sleep without you.
You're going to leave me so blue.
What in the hell will I do.
I'll just cry Johnny - Cry Johnny cry!

cc: Fred de Cordova
cc: Doc Severinson
cc: Tonight Show Coordinator

(OVER)

Chapter Thirteen **Poems**

We opened more poems than we could count,

Toward the end, they continued to mount.

Some were sad and made us cry,

Some just said, "Johnny, good-bye!"

As far as prose, there was no drought,

Some poems rhymed and some didn't...

Johnny touched hearts and inspired creativity all across the land.

" Sing to the tune of "Oh Johnny"

Oh Johnny

Oh Johnny, Oh Johnny
Say it's not true.
Oh Johnny, Oh Johnny
How I'll miss you.
I spend my nights in ecstacy.
With my remote, a beer and good old N.B.C. eeee-----

Oh Johnny, Oh Johnny
What will I do.
I can't go to sleep without you.
You're going to leave me so blue.
What in the hell will I do.
I'll just cry Oh Johnny - Cry Johnny Cry! "

He was never afraid of the stakes as he handled Jim Fowler's deadly snake.
Doing his President Reagan impersonation, caused quite a sensation
As for the jokes in the Political Arena, they took our minds off all
the seriousness and tensions in life and we laughed like some Hyena!
And when you portrayed several make-believe and unforgettable characters
Such as Art Fern, King Tut, Floyd Turbo Jr., Carmack the Magnificent and
El Moldo showing the Ham in Ya!!!
It not only gave us hours of hilarious entertainment, but it also
Enhanced us as to your various Comic Stamina!!!
Although there have been many Talk Show Hosts before and after you
Merv Griffin, Joey Bishop. Jack Parr, Dick Cavett, David Frost, Joan Rivers
Alan Thicke, David Brenner, Pat Sajak, David Letterman, Jay Leno and
Arsenio Hall
You have outlasted and surpassed them ALL!!
You are quite Unique, a combination of Charisma, Comedic Charm and
Ability and Tact.
That has proven to be a well known and unanimous Fact!!
ALL American as Home-Made Apple Pie
I truly believe that irregardless of all the Fame and Fortune plus all
the Adulation of Monumental Presentations and Ovations
Here-in underlies a Real sweet, sincere and Down to Earth Guy!!!
As the final Curtain [redacted] on T.V.'s greatest Career Closes
It is with utmost Respect, Admiration and Devotion, your Life exposes
Johnny, although I don't profess to be any Poet Laureate,
I want you to know these words are merely a part.
Of the sincere sentiment that comes straight from my Heart!!!

With Love & Best Wishes,

"He was never afraid of the stakes as he handled Jim Fowler's deadly snakes doing his President Reagan impersonation, caused quite a sensation.

As for the jokes in the Political Arena, they took our minds off all the seriousness and tensions in life and we laughed like some Hyena!

And when you/he portrayed several make-believe and unforgettable characters such as Art Fern, King Tut, Floyd Turbo Jr., [Carmack] the Magnificent and El Moldo showing the Ham in Ya!!!

It not only gave us hours of hilarious entertainment, but it also enhanced us as to your various Comic Stamina!!!

Although there have been many Talk Show Hosts before and after you, Merv Griffin, Joey Bishop, Jack Parr, Dick Cavett, David Frost, Joan Rivers, Alan Thicke, David Brenner, Pat Sajack, David Letterman, Jay Leno and Arsenio Hall.

You have outlasted and surpassed them all!!

You are quite unique, a combination of Charisma, Comedic Charm and Ability and Tact.

That has proven to be a well known and unanimous fact!!

All American as Home-made Apple Pie.

I truly believe that irregardless of all the Fame and Fortune plus all the [adjulation] of monumental presentations and ovations.

[Here-in] underlies a real sweet, sincere and Down to Earth Guy !!!

As the final Curtain on T.V.'s greatest career closes

It is with utmost respect, admiration and devotion, your life exposes Johnny, although I don't profess to be any Poet Laureate, I want you to know these words are merely a part.

Of the sincere sentiment that comes straight from my Heart!!!"

CARSON COLLEGE

After thirty years in Carson's College,
we had lots of laughs and gained some knowlege
of what makes Johnny run.
We've seen all the stars, (some straight from bars)
and most of them good jolly fun.
They introduced the other kind,
that really made us use our mind,
when Sagan told of bewions and bewions more.
No, not the stars of Hollywood,
or TV fame, it's understood,
but stars born in Creations core.

Without reason or rhyme,
they lessened show time,
a reduction of forty-five minutes.
To keep it all right,
we still watched TONIGHT,
the hour with far less within it.
Just Don Adams' beginning,
and Mark Spitz after winning,
the gold after multiple gold.
From two Judds among others
to brothers named Smothers,
and Don Rickles - surprisingly bold.

We heard lots of jokes,
from many old folks,
whose minds were eternally young.
We saw writers and singers,
and even bell ringers,
whose bells were artistically rung.
Joan Embry we've seen,
bring beasts that she'd screened,
yet still made Johnny a mess.
Big Ed gave the gaff,
with his big hearty laugh,
and gargled his gravelly, "YES".

WHEREEEEEEE'S JOHNNY?

Just look at this contraption, they call it a tv set,
It has dials and knobs and a little glass face
Lord, what'll they think of next?

As I approach it with caution
And turn the knob to 'on'
I hear a funny noise,
Reckon I did something wrong?

The glass face starts to flicker
I see wavy lines and snow
Then I hear a voice from deep within,
Stay tune for the CARSON show!

Well I step back, take a sip of my beer,
And stare in disbelief
I think I see a man in there
But lord, how can that be?

As the wavy lines continue
And the snow keeps falling down,
I hear music from a band somewhere
And there's laughter all around

At first I think that there's a parade,
Or the circus has come to town
Then I realize it's coming from that little box
My god, you could'a knocked me down!

The number from the dial says four,
But that means nothing to me
The wonderful part is the picture
On this thing they call a tv.

But they must be in Alaska
In the middle of a storm
And that Carson fella, an Eskimo
Is the funniest guy in town.

Sometimes I see his body
But you can't make out his face
It's hid behind those curvy lines
And that snow, all over the place.

But maybe someday they'll per-fect this thing,
That they call a tv set
Then I can see this Johnny Carson
And that fella, Ed McMahon.

WHEREEEEEE'S JOHNNY?

March 1992

Dear Johnny

I really love your monologues
Although some are pretty bad
The kooky characters in your skit
Can also be pretty sad.

But, Johnny
I have to tell you
How much you have meant to me
You've made this insomniac happy
By being on T.V.

You've shared my bed for thirty years
But, please do not disparage
No alimony is due me
As it was just a convenience marriage

Stay well, stay happy, stay married
Be all that you can be
The first two are quite easy
But, (as you know) divorces are not free

And, so old friend I say adieu
I'm going to miss you much
Please do a couple of "specials"
Just to stay in touch.

Good Luck, good health, much happiness in all that you endeaver

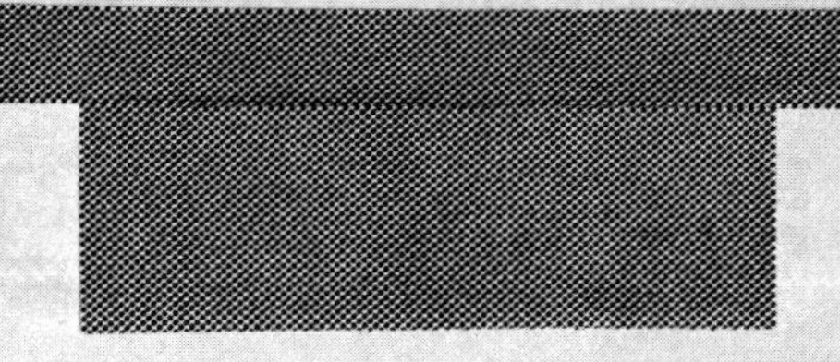

JOHNNY CARSON

J is for the jokes that made us laugh
throughout the years.
O is for the other ones that bombed and
brought you tears.
H is for your humor and great sense of
style.
N is for the numerous times you make us
smile.
N is for the never-ending pride our country
boasts.
Y because you're loved by everyone from
coast to coast.

C is for the concern that you show every
guest.
A is for the admiration that makes you the
very best.
R is for the reruns that will always entertain.
S is for the stage on which we wish you
would remain.
O is for the ovation you will get May
twenty-two.
N because no one will ever do it like you
do!

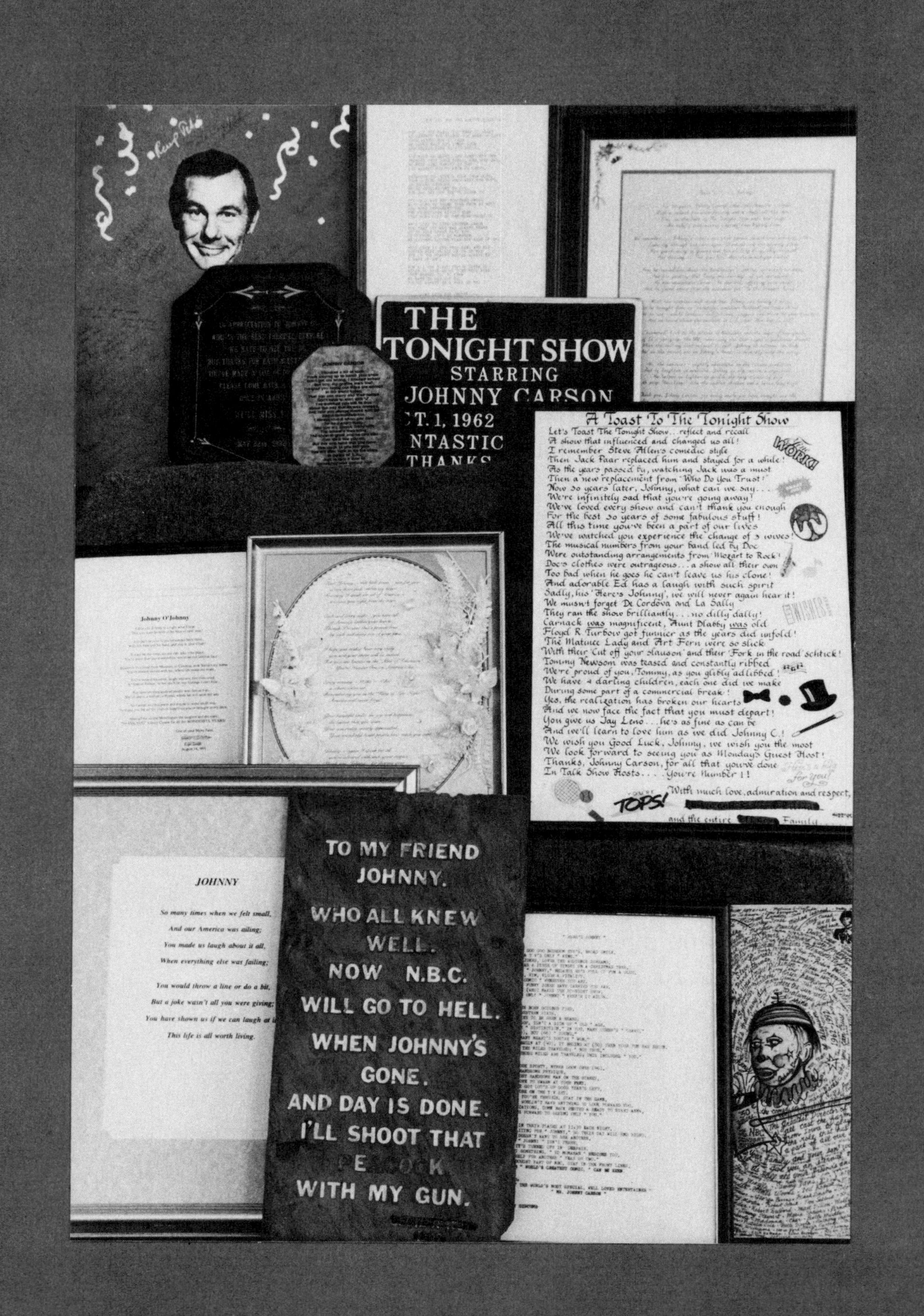
THE TONIGHT SHOW
STARRING
JOHNNY CARSON
A Toast To The Tonight Show
Let's Toast The Tonight Show... reflect and recall
A show that influenced and changed us all!
I remember Steve Allen's comedic style
Then Jack Paar replaced him and stayed for a while!
As the years passed by, watching Jack was a must
Then a new replacement from "Who Do You Trust!"
Now 30 years later, Johnny, what can we say...
We're infinitely sad that you're going away!
We've loved every show and can't thank you enough
For the best 30 years of some fabulous stuff!
All this time you've been a part of our lives
We've watched you experience the change of 3 wives!
The musical numbers from your band led by Doc
Were outstanding arrangements from Mozart to Rock!
Doc's clothes were outrageous... a show all their own
Too bad when he goes he can't leave us his clone!
And adorable Ed has a laugh with such spirit
Sadly, his 'Here's Johnny', we will never again hear it!
We mustn't forget De Cordova and La Sally
They ran the show brilliantly... no dilly dally!
Carnack was magnificent, Aunt Blabby was old
Floyd R. Turbow got funnier as the years did unfold!
The Matinee Lady and Art Fern were so slick
With their 'Cut off your Slauson' and their 'Fork in the road' schtick!
Tommy Newsom was teased and constantly ribbed
We're proud of you, Tommy, as you glibly adlibbed!
We have 4 darling children, each one did we make
During some part of a commercial break!
Yes, the realization has broken our hearts
And we now face the fact that you must depart!
You give us Jay Leno... he's as fine as can be
And we'll learn to love him as we did Johnny C.!
We wish you Good Luck, Johnny, we wish you the most
We look forward to seeing you as Monday's Guest Host!
Thanks, Johnny Carson, for all that you've done
In Talk Show Hosts.... You're Number 1!
TOPS!
With much love, admiration and respect,
Johnny O'Johnny
JOHNNY
So many times when we felt small,
And our America was ailing;
You made us laugh about it all,
When everything else was failing;
You would throw a line or do a bit,
But a joke wasn't all you were giving;
This life is all worth living.
TO MY FRIEND
JOHNNY.
WHO ALL KNEW
WELL.
NOW N.B.C.
WILL GO TO HELL.
WHEN JOHNNY'S
GONE.
AND DAY IS DONE.
I'LL SHOOT THAT
WITH MY GUN.

Poems and engraved plaques came to our office every day, but some really stood out.

- **The second item from the top middle is an actual grave marker to convey this viewer's deep feeling about Johnny's retirement.**
- **The second poem from the bottom left was created on a stone tablet which weighs over 20 lbs.**

Dear Johnny,

I can't believe that our 30 years together are soon to be over. When you first started in 1962 I was just 17 and working my first job at a nursing home. I worked the 3-11 shift and would come home from work, put my feet up and along with my mother would watch you till 1:00 am. Oh what a grand time you gave us!

As I grew older, got married, had my children you were still there, giving me "class" entertainment. As I sat feeding my babies at midnight you kept me company, or as I rocked one of them when they were sick you helped me stay awake. As the years passed and we grew older I have to admit, I grew sleepier! I wasn't always faithful, I just

Chapter Fourteen **Good-Bye Johnny - We'll Miss You**

Only those who worked for the "Tonight Show" could describe what the last couple of months were like before Johnny retired. Every day seemed to be a media event. Television news crews and reporters became fixtures in the "Tonight Show" office. Reporters toting cameras and equipment were staked out in the

"I can't believe that our 30 years together are soon to be over. When you first started in 1962 I was just 17 and working my first job at a nursing home. I worked the 3-11 shift and would come home from work, put my feet up and along with my mother would watch you till 1:00 a.m. Oh what a grand time you gave us!

As I grew older, got married, had my children you were still there, giving me "class" entertainment. As I sat feeding my babies at midnight you kept me company, or as I rocked one of them when they were sick you helped me stay awake. As the years passed and we grew older I have to admit, I grew sleepier! I wasn't always faithful, I just couldn't keep my eyes open past 11:00, so I watched you less and less, although many nights I had good intentions. Now you are leaving me and I feel sad and very nostalgic. Now I won't have a reason to try and stay up late anymore... I'll miss the challenge of the heavy eyelids!

I wish for you all good things, you truly are a legend.

Thanks a million for all our years together... Could I now qualify for alimony?

Fondly,"

hallways. The phones were ringing off the hook as callers hoped to get one of those final tickets, that last-minute interview, the final guest list or just an

Mr. Johnny Carson
NBC Studios
Burbank, CA

Dear Mr. Carson;

Many people wonder, as they look back on a career, if their work has made a difference. I am writing this letter to let you know that your work has made a difference in at least one life -- mine.

The summer I was ten was a long, lonely, frightening summer. My father's alcoholism was at it's peak and I was being sexually, physically, and emotionally abused. My mother worked late and seldom returned home before midnight. There was very little laughter in my life. But at 10:30, after I was supposed to be asleep and Dad had passed out, I would sneak downstairs. I pulled a large chair very close to our black and white television and turned the volume on very low. And for an hour and a half each night, Mr. Carson, you brought laughter into the life of a sad, battered little girl. Of course I couldn't laugh out loud. That would have been too dangerous. But I laughed on the inside and healed a little during those brief respites.

It was those little oases in a childhood of grief -- like the one you gave me the summer I was 10 -- that have allowed me to survive my troubled youth to become a functioning adult. And now when I watch you it's safe to laugh aloud. And sometimes I laugh so loud that my children and husband look at me a little oddly. But mostly they just smile. Because they know how long that laughter was silenced. Thank you, Mr. Carson. Thank you so much for the gift of laughter. And best of luck as you move on to new adventures.

Love and deep gratitude,

opportunity to share their heartfelt thoughts about the imminent change in their lives due to Johnny's retirement.

As the day of his departure approached, there was a media fire storm. "Life," "TV Guide," "Entertainment Weekly," and "People" magazines were just a few of the publications paying tribute to Johnny's three-decade command of his late night institution.

No one could have possibly predicted the tonnage of mail that would deluge NBC when Johnny announced that May 22, 1992 was to be his last night as host of the "Tonight Show." The mail seemed to ooze out of the walls. Ordinarily, we would have one to three bins filled with letters in our office, but now it was more like five and six. The job of opening it all seemed daunting. Video and audio cassette deliveries quadrupled as those aspiring to get their big break on the show, knowing time was limited, needed to request a guest spot immediately. The portraits and the paintings began to stack up. We were receiving poems framed and mounted as well as greeting cards the size of Rhode Island. Toys, gifts, new food products (and fruitcakes), more art work, clothing, and a megalithic amount of flower arrangements seemed to take over our office.

Mr. Johnny Carson
NBC Studios
Burbank, Ca.

Dear Mr. Carson,

News of your retirement has motivated me to write to you.

I remember when your show first aired and my mother would not let me stay up to watch. When I heard adults talking about your show I would try to finegle a way to sneak out into the living room just to see your show. I could hardly wait until I was old enough to stay up that late. Fortunatly for me, my mother punished me by making me move to the basement. We had an old television down there, which I put to good use watching your show almost every night!

I have continued to be an avid fan of yours through the years and am really sorry to see you retire. Your type of comedy is what I like. The new late night shows are a bit weird. I would not be surprised to hear that most viewers my age feel the same way. I realize the stations must cater to the buying public and most late night viewers are younger than me. I do represent a large group of your fans which, unfortunatly, can not stay awake late like we used to! I wish you would stay on and move your show up an hour!

Mr. Carson, I will always remember the laughter and enjoyment you brought into my life. I hope to meet you some day.

Thank you for reading my letter.

Sincerely,

The entire NBC facility was buzzing. Ticket-holders camped out for days in fear they would lose their place in line and miss one of Johnny's last shows. It was a hectic time, filled with such excitement and such incredible ambivalence about the future. It was difficult to believe that May 22nd would ever really arrive, that television history was soon to take place. The last week was like a huge party, but you knew you had to face reality and start to clean out your desk.

Now, only days away from Johnny's last appearance, the number of letters peaked. Practically every letter was a brief history of the sender's life in terms of how Johnny changed it, saved it, or just made it happier. We read about entire generations who passed along the Tonight-Show-watching tradition to their children. Some of our "regular writers" seriously worried about the forthcoming void in their lives. School children, baby-boomers, senior citizens, the well-off, the struggling, and all of America poured out their souls to attempt to convey their feelings about losing Carnac, Aunt Blabby, Floyd R. Turbo, Tea Time Movie's Art Fern, and all the other characters Johnny brought to life. But they probably just felt like they were losing a lifelong friend.

Dear Mr. Carson;

I'm writing to you to let you know that my family and I will miss you dearly when you leave the show.

But we understand that its time to move on and wish you and your family all the best in the coming years.

This is also a thank you letter for what you have done for my family over the years.

In October of 1978, you even saved my families and my LIFE. We were watching your show when a fire broke out in our home. If it wasn't for the fact that we never miss your show we would have been in bed and asleep when the fire started. I dread to think what might have happened if it weren't for you.

Thank you again for all the years of joy and happiness you have given my family.

P.S. Give our love to Ed, Doc, The Band, and Crew of your show.

P.S.S. Please forgive the typewritten letter, my hand writting is unreadable.

America loved Johnny Carson. He was truly the nation's night light for nearly thirty years. He became a friend to the lonely, court jester to the sick, and imaginary lover to those who longed for companionship. He was the barometer for the climate of the culture, and he enhanced many lives by helping humanity feel better about the world and themselves... for at least an hour every night.

Johnny Carson
c/o NBC
Hollywood CA

Dear Johnny

I want to thank you for appearing on you show January 10 of this year. I do believe you saved my life. I arrived home that night and had something to eat then decided to watch TV for a while. Well ten minutes into the show I had a mild stroke affected my left arm and leg.

Not being a fan of Jay Leno I had decided if he were on in your place I would go to bed. Because you were appearing I sat down to watch the show so I was immediately aware of my affliction and was able to seek timely medical attention. I really believe that had I gone to bed I and thus unaware of my situation I would have been more seriously affected by the attack.

As it is I am now out of the hospital for a week and I am on my way to hopefully a full recovery. So thanks again for showing up that night and best wishes for all your future plans.

JOHNNY CARSON
C/O N. B. C.
3000 WEST ALAMEDA AVE.
BURBANK, CA. 91523

Dear Johnny,

I feel deprived. I have withdrawl pains. I am feeling actually ill. I am an addict of "Here Comes Johnny" and have been for thirty years and I am also filled with dispair at your leaving.

I am a senior citizen but not when I put on Channel 4 at 11:00 P. M. This is my security blanket to ease and relax thetension at the end of a long day.After 1½ hours in former years and 1 hour now,looking at you so handsome; so debonair; your impeccable suits and ties; your "shtick" with your eyes; matched only by Jack Benny; your self , sophisticated repatee with the lovely ladies; your brilliant comment on politcks; world events; people in the news; you are an encyclopedia of information. No matter how obscure the subject matter your guests bring up, you are never at a loss for words. You are the stimulant that tranqualizes me at the end of the day.

When Franklin D. Roosevelt and John F. Kenedy left, I mourned with deep heartache the losses in my life. You Know, Johnny,it's like someone in my own family: and although you are very much alive: you will not be current or daily as before. I realize how selfish this is of me, because actually I want to thank you , as does the the whole world for making our lives happier and more exiciting. Your fans love you. You are an original; irreplacable by anyone. Please have many specials and soon. I wish you health and happiness.

P, S. I would appreciate and love to have a picture. In my excitement I forgot to thank Ed McMahn. He is quite a figure even in your shadow.

Dear Mr. Carson,

Hello! My name is [redacted] I am a 37 year old housewife from [redacted], and an avid fan of your show.

My Mother has always taught me to write thank you notes for gifts I have received. Since I have been enjoying the gift of your show for most of the 30 years you have been on the air, I felt that a thank you note to you was more than in order.

I know you hate to hear this, but I used to sneak down the stairs as a small girl to listen to your show as my parents watched. I knew I had arrived into adulthood when my parents let me stay up on a non-school night to watch your show! My brother, three sisters and I would pop pop-corn and settle in for 1½ hours and then 1 hour of pure entertainment.

When my childre were small and I was too exhausted to stay up and watch you, I would record your show and Late Night With David Lettermanon my VCR (which by the way I CAN program),and watch your shows during the afternoon while my children napped. I would later share exerpts from your shows with my husband and children.

When I quit my teaching job to atay home with my children, I vowed that I would never watch Soap Operas. I told my husband that if he ever caught me watching them, to shoot me ! I figured if I had gone that far, I didn't deserve to live!

My husband and I will be married 16 years on June 26, and I've always teased him that there are only two other men in my life, Johnny and David (Letterman)!

My only regret is that we never made it out to see your show in person.

I have one small request: Would you PLEASE do Carnac one more time? He is my absolute favorite character!

Thank you, Mr. Carson, for 30 years of excellence! You will be greatly missed!

Enclosed is a picture of my family.

With Sincere Best Wishes,

Johnny Carson
% The Tonight Show
3000 W. Alameda Avenue
Burbank, CA 91523

Dear John,

I was so sorry to hear of the death of your son, but something important happened that I felt you should know.

On the night that you talked about your son and showed his wonderful pictures, you saved my family's lives. I had fallen asleep at approximately 12:10 A.M. when that show was on. Somehow, my subconcious heard you discussing your son, and I woke up to listen. What you did was very touching and loving. You are right, driver license pictures should not be the picture people should remember. Anyway, I heard water rushing somewhere in the house, but I did not recall haveing turned on any water source. I got up to investigate, and found the hose to the washihg machine had burst. The rushihg water had put the pilot light out to the water heater. Gas was escaping into the house. I was able to turn off the gas source and the water line to the house. If you had not given your son the attention he deserved, My family and I might not be here right now. Thank you, if ever so inadvertantly, for saving our lives. On August 5th, I delivered a beautiful baby girl, bringing the total number of children in mhouse to four.

Your son was very talented. Thank you for showing his photographs and touching my heart. I, too, have suffered unexpected loss. Your segment allowed me to again remember my losses fondly.

As an added postscript, I went to Piedmont High School, and always got to see the yearly Bird Calling contest. This was before it was so difficult to get a ticket (though I have one in my scrapbook). It is great to see my old teacher Mr. Waxdeck every year. I hope Jay continues to show the students every year as you have done.

Sincerely,

Mr. Johnny Carson
NBC
3000 W. Alameda Ave.
Burbank, Ca. 91523

Dear Johnny:

Many, many years ago, when I was a lad of fourteen and you were not yet on the Tonight Show, I used to rush home from junior high, make myself a quick mayonnaise and mustard sandwich, and turn on Who Do You Trust?

I lived in Pompano Beach at the time and you used to vacation in Fort Lauderdale; on one of your visits I went down to the hotel where you were staying, determined somehow to meet my idol, and asked what room you were in — pretty gutsy for a young kid! I called your room on the house phone and was told very politely by somebody that you were busy. Ah. . .but I was determined to meet you, so I called my mother and told her I was going to wait in the lobby of the hotel. . .all night, if necessary!. . . since I knew you eventually had to come down!

Well, in a couple of hours, you did, and I rushed forward with my little Kodak, licking my little flash bulb. . .and I will never forget your graciousness in stopping your entourage to let me take your picture! I was thunderstruck by your taking time to talk to me and was on a high for days; I sent the picture to you, which you returned, autographed.

The treasured pictures went into a photo album which I made, and, having recently come across them again, I made some copies of the pages and am enclosing them; the little blurb, if my memory serves me, is from TV Guide.

At any rate, like the countless millions who will sorely miss you next month, Johnny, I wish you well and thank you for thirty years of really great stuff! I treasure these pictures and will always remember your kindness so long ago with a kid who thought you were a pretty cool guy. . .and still does!

Again. . .all the best!

Yours truly,

Dear Mr. Carson,

I have never written a fan letter in my life. But with your up coming retirement from your show, I just could not let you leave without writing.

Whether you know it or not you have been a role model for me and many people of my age group (41) which by the way you've by your own example and the guest you have had on over the years prove age is so relative in how you look at yourself and live. Anyway! the way you have presented your self, finding humor in most things (damm, those Lincoln jokes are still tough), not taking yourself too serious, but taking the quality of your show so, has been a great example. Your effort to find interest in so many people and things has taught me the same thing.

I started watching your show in 1964 when I was in the seventh grade, on the sly with the volume low, but your message over the years of looking for the positive side of things came through loud and clear. Quite frankly when things were rather tough on my side of the screen I found a nightly consistency of an attitude of what ever is going on in the world, you can make it, keep your chin up, things can and will get better if you try, and for that I say THANK YOU and for so many other reasons, it would take pages and I can tell it makes you feel uncomfortable when folks go on and on, besides I choke up easy. So in closing let me just say you have been a positive influence in my life and I will miss you, Please don't stay away from the tube too long. Someone once said, television is a cultural wasteland, if so, you have always been an oasis. Please take care.

Peace and Plenty,

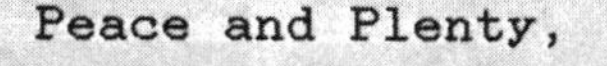

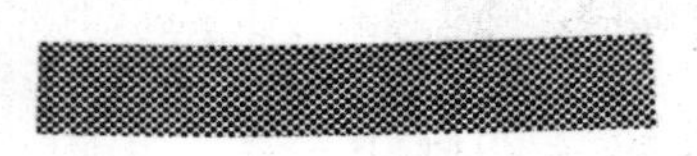

Mr. Johnny Carson
The Tonight Show
NBC
3000 West Alameda Avenue
Burbank, CA 91523

Dear Mr. Carson:

As you draw to the close of your Tonight Show tenure, I would like to sincerely thank you for all of the enjoyment you have provided over the past three decades. I doubt you think of this, but you and I (as well as thousands of Tonight Show viewers) have come a long way together.

I was on hand as a youngster, sneaking downstairs in a darkened house to turn on the TV in defiance of parents' orders, to see Ed Ames hatchet throw. You, or rather Carnac, brought me THE biggest laugh of my life -- the "Sss, boom, bah" answer to the question "What is the sound made by an exploding sheep?" I howelled (and quietly identified) with Mickey Rooney's comment on the world being a tux and him feeling like a pair of brown shoes. And I roared again as Joan Embry and others brought wild animals to the show, knowing that each show would result in at least one close call with a set of teeth or leaky bladder.

Your show help me recover from the misery of the Kennedy assasination; from more than one foundered relationship; from the rigors of the draft lottery; from hundreds of tough days at work; and from dispare when my Grandmother passed. You never disappointed.

Though the past years for you have been demanding and -- as I have recently read -- often not easy, I appreciate and respect your perseverance and dedication to making me and millions of others forget our trials and traumas.

Best wishes for an enjoyable retirement. If I could write your pension checks, I'd make them big ones for you have given all you could to your audiences...and to me.

Sincerely,

5.11.92

Johnny Carson
The Tonight Show
NBC Burbank

While discussing your departure from the Tonight Show I mentioned to a few of my associates what I believed to be the quintessential final scene. During the past few days I have received several calls urging me to send this to you.

When there is about five minutes of air time left you should thank the public for accepting you into their homes, bedrooms and hearts for the past thirty years. While all the celebrity accolades of the past month are heart warming the outpouring of affection from your audience should be acknowledged. When about two minutes of air time are left you should say goodnight. The set should fade to black and a single spot should light the FATTEST FEMALE OPERA SINGER you can find. She should begin to sing an opera with no musical arrangement. The show is over... The tonight show band is silenced... The fat lady has sung.

Don't tell the audience what they are seeing. Let them see it, hear it and figure it out themselves. The totally cool way you said good-bye will be part of television history.

Hope you like it. Please use it. I would add my two cents by saying thank-you. For the record, a few years ago an elderly woman was on the show and mentioned how she had very old and worn out appliances. I for one never liked you any better than when you told her, in front of me, that you would send her new appliances. I was proud of you then and you raised yourself above the celebrity you enjoy.

Good luck in your next career,

THE FAT LADY COULD BE ROSEANN BARR ARNOLD!

Mr. Johnny Carson
THE TONIGHT SHOW
NBC Studios
Burbank, California

Dear Mr. Carson:

I've thought a long time about writing this letter. A thank you letter should be written promptly, and I apologize for my procrastination. I could have written this letter in 1962, or 1966, or 1969. I could have written it in 1970, or 1975, or 1980. I just never took the time, and perhaps that was for the best in one sense, since its meaning wasn't clear-- how much thanks I owed you wasn't evident-- until my Grandfather died in 1981..

I was very close to my Granddad. I called him Pap. And my Pap and I used to watch the TONIGHT SHOW regularly. When I visited, he and I would sit up late. We'd laugh at your monologues. We'd share comments about your guests. He'd smoke his pipe and disagree with you occasionally. Then we'd laugh at Karnak, or Carol Wayne, or you and Ed McMahon. We spent a lot of valuable time that way. We shared time that now is just a memory. And I hear him laughing, and talking, and I almost smell that pipe.

Thank you, Mister Carson, for providing this grandson those memories. I was very sorry to hear about your own son, and I'm sure the TONIGHT SHOW has not always been wine and roses for you. We in the audience tend to forget the personal toll the limelight can take. The papers tend to make tragedies their selling points. I hope this small thank you cuts through some of those slights. I do appreciate very much the time you gave me and my Pap.

Good luck always:

From all of your loving fans

"Good-bye Johnny. Indeed, we'll miss you… "